JESUS AND THE DISINHERITED

JESUS
and the Disinherited

Howard Thurman

Foreword by Vincent Harding

BEACON PRESS
BOSTON

Beacon Press
25 Beacon Street
Boston, Massachusetts 02108-2892
www.beacon.org

Beacon Press books
are published under the auspices of
the Unitarian Universalist Association of Congregations.

First published 1949 by Abingdon Press

This book is printed on acid-free paper that meets the
uncoated paper ANSI/NISO specifications for permanence
as revised in 1992.

11 10 09 08 07   16 15 14 13

Library of Congress Cataloging-in-Publication Data

Thurman, Howard, 1900-1981.
Jesus and the disinherited / Howard Thurman ; foreward by
Vincent Harding.
p.   cm.
Originally published: New York, Abingdon-Cokesbury Press,
1949. Includes bibliographical references and index.
ISBN 978-0-8070-1029-7
1. Jesus Christ-Teachings. 2. Sociology, Biblical. I. Title.
BS2417.S7T5   1996
261.8'3456-dc20   96-21205

To
My Beloved Daughters
OLIVE and ANNE

and to the future of their generation
in whom the struggles of the
past will find fulfillment

Foreword

A superficial encounter with the title of Howard Thurman's classic statement, *Jesus and the Disinherited*, could easily lead us to anticipate a 1940s version of liberation theology, with its now familiar message that God is on the side of the oppressed, with its powerful and prophetic condemnation of the oppressors and their cruel systems of dehumanization, with its urgent calls to repentance, resistance, and hope. But nothing in Thurman's large and magnificently varied body of work ever yielded itself to superficial readings, and this invaluable half-century-old text is no exception.

For although it is possible to glean elements of a liberation theology from its pages, this richly endowed, seminal work can be more accurately and helpfully described as a profound quest for a liberating spirituality, a way of exploring and experiencing those crucial life points where personal and societal transformation are creatively joined. It is the centerpiece of the Black prophet-mystic's lifelong attempt to bring the harrowing beauty of the African-American experience into deep engagement with what he called "the religion of Jesus." Ultimately his goal was to offer this humanizing combination as the basis for an emancipatory way of being, moving toward a fundamentally unchained life that is available to all the women and men everywhere who hunger and thirst for righteousness, especially those "who stand with their backs against the wall."

Stating his central intention in a slightly different way, early in the book Thurman said that he had written for "those who need profound succor and strength to enable them to live in the present with dignity and creativity." Still, the great teacher, preacher, and sage never strayed far from his basic urgent metaphor of the wall. Repeatedly he announced that he was attempting to explore and explain "what the teachings of Jesus have to say to those who stand at a moment in human history with their backs against the wall . . . the poor, the disinherited, the dispossessed." In essence he was surveying the world of the oppressed and asking how it might be possible for human beings to endure the terrible pressures of the dominating world without losing their humanity, without forfeiting their souls.

For Thurman this project was no distanced, merely intellectual task. (Of course, no work of his ever took on that character.) At the outset he made it clear that his interest in the issues "has been and continues to be both personal and professional." Born into the Black community of Daytona Beach, Florida, at the beginning of the century, he was carefully nurtured by a maternal grandmother who had come through the fierce crucible of slavery while "leaning on the Lord." So Thurman possessed an intimate knowledge of the harsh contours and consequences of America's walls as well as a profound appreciation for the amazing inner resources of those people who had stood firmly against the hardness without losing their humanity or betraying their souls. And there was never any doubt in his mind that the life and teachings of Jesus, "the poor Jew" of Nazareth, the disinherited, threatened subject of Roman power, were especially relevant to the ever-present contingent of Black men and women who lined the serrated, cutting surfaces of the wall called America. So he could unhesitatingly declare that "the striking similarity between the social position of Jesus in Palestine and that of the vast majority of American Negroes is obvious to anyone who tarries long over the facts."

Thurman had been tarrying over and wrestling with these urgent matters for most of his adult life. He took the concerns with him when he left Florida in 1919 to attend Morehouse College in Atlanta, and was able to discuss them with fellow students such as Martin Luther King, Sr., faculty members such as Benjamin E. Mays and E. Franklin Frazier, and the visionary president of the school, John Hope. The issues and questions were unavoidably on his mind as he moved on to engage the world of white theological education at Rochester Theological Seminary in upstate New York. And they were clearly even more crucial to his life in 1935 when, from his important base at Howard University's Rankin Chapel, Thurman published the seven-page essay "Good News for the Underprivileged" in the prestigious ecumenical journal *Religion in Life*. It was that essay that became the essential core of *Jesus and the Disinherited* when the book was first published in 1949.

The post–World War II years were, of course, a crucial transitional period in the history of African-Americans. New beginnings in politics, economics, and human migration were being shaped by and for Black America, and a new contingent of leaders was expressing its determination to break the power of Jim Crow, the legalized—and terrorizing—system of segregation that formed the structural core of America's brutal wall. Thurman and his writings moved regularly, influentially among this group of "New Negroes." At the same time he often served as pastor, preacher, and retreat leader for many of the increasing number of white men and women who sought some source of alliance with the fermenting Black forces.

Crucial to the sense of change that marked the African-American community by the end of the 1940s was its acute awareness of the rising tide of anticolonial struggles that was shaking the foundations of white, Western world hegemony in places such as Africa, India, and Asia. Thurman was a part of all that, and the "Disinherited" of his title was also meant to encompass the colonized peoples beyond these shores. (Indeed, shortly after "Good News for the Underprivileged" was published, Thurman and his gifted soul mate, wife, and coworker, Sue Bailey Thurman, were visiting with Gandhi in India, seeking to learn from the Mahatma's experiences in spiritually based social struggle and responding to his well-informed questions about the African-American situation.)

When *Jesus and the Disinherited* appeared the Thurmans had already left Howard University, and Howard Thurman was serving as pastor of the nation's first intentionally interracial congregation, the Church for the Fellowship of All People in San Francisco. By that time Thurman had developed an approach to (or better, a relationship with) Jesus of Nazareth that took him beyond the central orthodoxies of American Christianity and, more importantly, was opening the way toward a liberating spirituality that made great demands on what he called the "inward center," the heart and soul of the dispossessed. For the spirituality that emerged and focused itself in *Jesus and the Disinherited* carried an insistent message that life under oppression provided no excuses for avoiding a path of courageous, creative integrity. As a matter of fact, while Thurman wrote with great compassion about the difficulties faced by the marginalized peoples whose lives are constantly besieged by the threatening, destructive power of the dominating forces, still this deeply loving and caring pastor of the dispossessed would not back away from the demands of a life of integrity, a life that refuses to give into "fear, hypocrisy and hatred, the three hounds of hell that track the trail of the disinherited." For he recognized—and he believed Jesus recognized—that no external force, however great and overwhelming, can at long last destroy a people if it does not first win the victory of the spirit against them."

In the light of that perspective it was not surprising that Thurman summarized the essential message of Jesus for the disinherited in these words: "You must abandon your fear of each other and fear only God. You must not indulge in any deception and dishonesty, even to save your lives. Your words must be Yea-Nea; anything else is evil. Hatred is destructive to hated and hater alike. Love your enemy, that you may be children of your father who is in heaven."

Throughout the work Thurman continued to hold his disinherited people to a magnificently (some would say unrealistically—but who defines the *real* within the mystery of "the inward center"?) high set of expectations. If it is true, as some accounts indicate, that Martin Luther King, Jr. often carried a copy of this text on his many journeys, then there are creative connections along the wall that may exceed even our greatest expectations. Of course, considering the generations-long relationships between the King and Thurman families, Martin likely had the message of these pages etched on his heart. It must have provided an important addition to his own resources when Black people constantly raised with him the question that was most directly articulated in the late 1960s by Stokely Carmichael (later Kwame Touré), that stalwart of the freedom movement who called the nation's attention to the bold and desperate cry for Black power. Not long before King's assassination in 1968 Stokely asked with mock innocence, "Dr. King, why do we have to be more moral than white folks?"

That question came out of a period when thousands of Black people were leaping away from the American wall and hurling angry, incendiary words and devices into the midst of the nation's life. When I realized that the first paperback edition of this work appeared in 1969, as the Black fires were only beginning to cool down, I wondered whether a contemporary generation of young people might possibly find any space in their lives for the firmly loving disciplines of the spirit that Thurman (and his friend, Jesus) press forward in this gift of a book. Then, just as I moved toward closing my work on this Foreword, I came across another gift, one that seemed to open the possibilities of a connection between Howard Thurman and a new generation of his (and my) children. Again the gift I found was a book, *Testimony*, a moving and impressive collection of essays and poetry edited by Natasha Tarpley and published in 1994. It was written by a group of some forty young African-American writers, most of whom were likely just entering elementary school when Thurman left us in the spring of 1981. What I sensed in their deeply reflective anthology was a level of integrity, self-examination, and social concern that would have brought one of those characteristically broad and deep smiles to the face of our father in the faith. (And when I noted that *Testimony* was also published by Beacon it seemed very likely that our dear mentor was up to one of his familiar creative tricks.)

Surely some of the gifted and committed young people of *Testimony* could find a vital connection with *Jesus and the Disinherited*, even if their walls are different from the ones Thurman and his grandmother knew. That is a cause for real joy, but much more has changed in this country than the character of the walls and the number of people who now escape their harsh pressures. So any serious reflection on the possible future of this landmark work from the past must take at least two of those essential changes into consideration.

First, we need to recall the fact that in the years when Thurman was most actively wrestling with the issues and spirits that emerged in *Jesus and the Disinherited*, the Black people who provided his major points of reference in this country often gathered in and around places and events where Jesus of Nazareth was celebrated and at least nominally recognized and followed. Today, at the close of Thurman's century, those people who live most obviously with their backs against the wall—for instance, the homeless, the working and jobless poor, the substance abused and abusers, the alienated, misguided, and essentially abandoned young people—are rarely within hearing or seeing range of the company of Jesus' proclaimed followers. The keepers of the faith of the master often find it very difficult, and very dangerous, to follow him into the hard places inhabited by the disinherited of America. And those wall-bruised people find no space for their presence in the places where the official followers are comfortably at worship, unless they happen to find themselves among such exceptions as the young, downwardly mobile worker-believers of the Azuza church fellowship in Dorchester, Massachusetts, or the interracial community of hope in Washington, D.C., the Abyssinian Sojourners.

On an even more complicated level, in this increasingly pluralistic nation Thurman's "religion of Jesus" and its strange mutation, American Christianity, are no longer considered the automatic, official possessors of any privileged monopoly on the truth of God or humanity. So Jesus' guidance for the disinherited may be available only through some direct, creative, perhaps disguised encounters between those whose wounded backs and spirits testify to the continuing reality of the walls and those who may no longer be forcibly pressed against them but who know the walls and the continuing struggle against the hounds of fear, hypocrisy, and hatred, and have determined to overcome. In unofficial, unprivileged, and dangerous encounters at the wall: perhaps that is the way Thurman would prefer us to meet his Jesus at the close of the twentieth century.

Of course, even in his somewhat less complicated time Thurman recognized that it would not be easy to develop models of hope from among the disinherited, and he quickly, quietly declared toward the end of his statement that "A profound piece of surgery has to take place in the very psyche of the disinherited before the great claim of the religion of Jesus can be presented. The great stretches of barren places in the soul must be revitalized, brought to life, before they can be challenged." Fortunately, he lived long enough to encounter a generation of pioneers in the 1960s (some of whom he had helped inspire) that was ready—at least for a time—to break away from the wall and take on the challenge of confrontation, healing, re-creation, and hope for themselves, for the nation, and for the world.

If he had continued in this life long enough to see Nelson Mandela walk in graceful triumph through the prison gates, away from the walls, Thurman would surely have recognized a living testimony to the power of the human spirit to overcome the hounds of fear, hypocrisy, and hatred, to resist the crippling calls for vengeance. In the light of such a life it may even be possible for us to return to the original 1935 pilot essay, to remember that the revitalization of the souls of the oppressed was never an end in itself for Thurman. For there, at the beginning of this long publishing path, the Black pilgrim reminded us of the larger social purposes of such creative disciplines of the spirit. Overlooking, or forgiving, his heavy tendency toward the male pronouns that were so much a part of his time, we are able to grasp Thurman's grandest contextual goal for the disinherited/underprivileged when he writes:

Often there are things on the horizon that point logically to a transformation of society, especially for the underprivileged, but he cannot co-operate with them because he is spiritually and intellectually confused. He mistakes fear for caution and caution for fear. Now, if his mind is free and his spirit unchained, he can work intelligently and courageously for a new day.

With Mandela as the great model of the unchained cocreator of a new day, with Malcolm as a suggestion of other liberated possibilities beyond the wall, beyond the chains, it is possible now to return to Stokely Carmichael's earlier question, and to recognize how crucial Thurman's work, Mandela's work, and Fannie Lou Hamer's work are to a full response. For such lives remind us that the ultimate issue is not being more moral than white folks, but becoming more free than we have ever been, free to engage our fullest powers in the transformative tasks that await us at the wall. As women and men moving toward our wholeness (our holiness?), we meet Thurman and the young people who are developing their *Testimony*. We meet Ella Baker and her Dorchester-loving children of Azuza. We meet countless others whose names and faces we have not seen, but know are real. We join our best young lives and rendezvous with Thurman, with his Jesus, and with all our departed and still-present veterans of the struggle for a new day. Finding unexpected companions everywhere (including at a Million Man March) whose backs and spirits will not be broken, whose lives are free to create new life, we discover why we must be more disciplined in love, integrity, and hope than anyone ever dreamed. There are new worlds to build, new visions to carry forward, new companions at the wall, new days to begin. Good morning, Howard Thurman.

A postmodern and postindustrial American postscript:
Although Thurman's message of the 1940s was focused on
the needs of the Black representatives of the disinherited in
the United States, by the last half of the final decade of the
twentieth century it is clear that his message is now replete
with significance for many other people as well. Latinos,
Native Americans, Southeast Asians, and many women and
gay and lesbian people are only the most obvious additions
to Thurman's community of the wall. For the pressures of
the postindustrialist capitalist world order have pushed
many other people against a great variety of unfamiliar and
unexpected walls (and glass ceilings), and we are all
hounded by the inner demons of fear, hypocrisy, and
hatred. So Thurman must be taken very seriously when he
still offers this work "for those who need profound succor
and strength to enable them to live in the present with dignity and creativity." Shall we gather at the wall?

VINCENT HARDING

Preface

THE significance of the religion of Jesus to people who stand with their backs against the wall has always seemed to me to be crucial. It is one emphasis which has been lacking—except where it has been a part of a very unfortunate corruption of the missionary impulse, which is, in a sense, the very heartbeat of the Christian religion. My interest in the problem has been and continues to be both personal and professional. This is the question which individuals and groups who live in our land always under the threat of profound social and psychological displacement face: Why is it that Christianity seems impotent to deal radically, and therefore effectively, with the issues of discrimination and injustice on the basis of race, religion and national origin? Is this impotency due to a betrayal of the genius of the religion, or is it due to a basic weakness in the religion itself? The question is searching, for the dramatic demonstration of the impotency of Christianity in dealing with the issue is underscored by its apparent inability to cope with it within its own fellowship.

I do not pretend that I have found an answer in the pages that follow; but I am deeply convinced that in the general area of my inquiry is to be found the answer without which there can be little hope that men may find in Christianity the fulfillment which it claims for its gospel.

It was in 1935, at the annual convocation of preaching at the School of Theology of Boston University, that I first gave formal shape to the basic idea in this study. Under the title "Good News for the Underprivileged," it was published as an article in *Religion in Life*, Summer, 1935. Subsequently the same ideas were developed in a prose poem on Jesus, "The Great Incarnate Words," which appeared in the magazine *Motive* in January, 1944. Later this prose poem was published as a part of a volume of poetic meditations under the title *The Greatest of These*. The comprehensive study of which this book is the full development was presented as the Mary L. Smith Memorial Lectures at Samuel Huston College, Austin, Texas, in April, 1948.

Appreciation is due and gladly acknowledged to Miss Grace E. Marrett and Miss Julia T. Lee for their patient checking of the manuscript for clarity and accuracy of expression; to Mrs. Aubrey Burns and Mrs. Virginia Scardigli for typing and retyping the manuscript; and to The Church for the Fellowship of All Peoples for the impetus.

HOWARD THURMAN

Contents

I.   JESUS–AN INTERPRETATION 11

II.   FEAR 36

III.   DECEPTION 58

IV.   HATE 74

V.   LOVE 89

EPILOGUE 110

CHAPTER ONE

Jesus
an Interpretation

To some God and Jesus may appeal in a way other than to us: some may come to faith in God and to love, without a conscious attachment to Jesus. Both Nature and good men besides Jesus may lead us to God. They who seek God with all their hearts must, however, some day on their way meet Jesus.[1]

MANY and varied are the interpretations dealing with the teachings and the life of Jesus of Nazareth. But few of these interpretations deal with what the teachings and the life of Jesus have to say to those who stand, at a moment in human history, with their backs against the wall.

To those who need profound succor and strength to enable them to live in the present with dignity and creativity, Christianity often has been sterile and of little avail. The conventional Christian word is muffled, confused, and vague. Too often the price exacted by society for security

[1] Heinrich Weinel and Alban G. Widgery, *Jesus in the Nineteenth Century and After*, p. 405.

11

and respectability is that the Christian movement in its formal expression must be on the side of the strong against the weak. This is a matter of tremendous significance, for it reveals to what extent a religion that was born of a people acquainted with persecution and suffering has become the cornerstone of a civilization and of nations whose very position in modern life has too often been secured by a ruthless use of power applied to weak and defenseless peoples.

It is not a singular thing to hear a sermon that defines what should be the attitude of the Christian toward people who are less fortunate than himself. Again and again our missionary appeal is on the basis of the Christian responsibility to the needy, the ignorant, and the so-called backward peoples of the earth. There is a certain grandeur and nobility in administering to another's need out of one's fullness and plenty. One could be selfish, using his possessions—material or spiritual—for strictly private or personal ends. It is certainly to the glory of Christianity that it has been most insistent on the point of responsibility to others whose only claim upon one is the height and depth of their need. This impulse at the heart of Christianity is the human *will to share* with others what one has found meaningful to oneself elevated to the height of a moral imperative. But there is a lurking danger in this very emphasis. It is exceedingly difficult to hold oneself free from a certain contempt for those whose predicament makes moral appeal for defense and succor. It is the sin of pride and arrogance that has tended to vitiate the missionary impulse and to make of it an instrument of self-righteousness on the one hand and racial superiority on the other.

That is one reason why, again and again, there is no basic relationship between the simple practice of brotherhood in the commonplace relations of life and the ethical pretensions of our faith. It has long been a matter of serious moment that for decades we have studied the various peoples of the world and those who live as our neighbors as objects of missionary endeavor and enterprise without being at all willing to treat them either as brothers or as human beings. I say this without rancor, because it is not an issue in which vicious human beings are involved. But it is one of the subtle perils of a religion which calls attention—to the point of overemphasis, sometimes—to one's obligation to administer to human need.

I can count on the fingers of one hand the number of times that I have heard a sermon on the meaning of religion, of Christianity, to the man who stands with his back against the wall. It is urgent that my meaning be crystal clear. The masses of men live with their backs constantly against the wall. They are the poor, the disinherited, the dispossessed. What does our religion say to them? The issue is not what it counsels them to do for others whose need may be greater, but what religion offers to meet their own needs. The search for an answer to this question is perhaps the most important religious quest of modern life.

In the fall of 1935 I was serving as chairman of a delegation sent on a pilgrimage of friendship from the students of America to the students of India, Burma, and Ceylon. It was at a meeting in Ceylon that the whole crucial issue was pointed up to me in a way that I can never forget. At the close of a talk before the Law College, University of Colombo, on civil disabilities under states' rights in the United States, I was invited by the principal to have coffee.

We drank our coffee in silence. After the service had been removed, he said to me, "What are you doing over here? I know what the newspapers say about a pilgrimage of friendship and the rest, but that is not my question. What are *you* doing over here? This is what I mean.

"More than three hundred years ago your forefathers were taken from the western coast of Africa as slaves. The people who dealt in the slave traffic were Christians. One of your famous Christian hymn writers, Sir John Newton, made his money from the sale of slaves to the New World. He is the man who wrote 'How Sweet the Name of Jesus Sounds' and 'Amazing Grace'—there may be others, but these are the only ones I know. The name of one of the famous British slave vessels was 'Jesus.'

"The men who bought the slaves were Christians. Christian ministers, quoting the Christian apostle Paul, gave the sanction of religion to the system of slavery. Some seventy years or more ago you were freed by a man who was not a professing Christian, but was rather the spearhead of certain political, social, and economic forces, the significance of which he himself did not understand. During all the period since then you have lived in a Christian nation in which you are segregated, lynched, and burned. Even in the church, I understand, there is segregation. One of my

14

students who went to your country sent me a clipping telling about a Christian church in which the regular Sunday worship was interrupted so that many could join a mob against one of your fellows. When he had been caught and done to death, they came back to resume their worship of their Christian God.

"I am a Hindu. I do not understand. Here you are in my country, standing deep within the Christian faith and tradition. I do not wish to seem rude to you. But, sir, I think you are a traitor to all the darker peoples of the earth. I am wondering what you, an intelligent man, can say in defense of your position."

Our subsequent conversation lasted for more than five hours. The clue to my own discussion with this probing, honest, sympathetic Hindu is found in my interpretation of the meaning of the religion of Jesus. It is a privilege, after so long a time, to set down what seems to me to be an essentially creative and prognostic interpretation of Jesus as religious subject rather than religious object. It is necessary to examine the religion of Jesus against the background of his own age and people, and to inquire into the content of his teaching with reference to the disinherited and the underprivileged.

We begin with the simple historical fact that Jesus was a Jew. The miracle of the Jewish people is almost as breathtaking as the miracle of Jesus. Is there something unique, some special increment of vitality in the womb of the people out of whose loins he came, that made of him a logical flowering of a long development of racial experience, ethi-

15

cal in quality and Godlike in tone? It is impossible for Jesus to be understood outside of the sense of community which Israel held with God. This does not take anything away from him; rather does it heighten the challenge which his life presents, for such reflection reveals him as the product of the constant working of the creative mind of God upon the life, thought, and character of a race of men. Here is one who was so conditioned and organized within himself that he became a perfect instrument for the embodiment of a set of ideals—ideals of such dramatic potency that they were capable of changing the calendar, rechanneling the thought of the world, and placing a new sense of the rhythm of life in a weary, nerve-snapped civilization.

How different might have been the story of the last two thousand years on this planet grown old from suffering if the link between Jesus and Israel had never been severed! What might have happened if Jesus, so perfect a flower from the brooding spirit of God in the soul of Israel, had been permitted to remain where his roots would have been fed by the distilled elements accumulated from Israel's wrestling with God! The thought is staggering. The Christian Church has tended to overlook its Judaic origins, but the fact is that Jesus of Nazareth was a Jew of Palestine when he went about his Father's business, announcing the acceptable year of the Lord.

Of course it may be argued that the fact that Jesus was a Jew is merely coincidental, that God could have expressed himself as easily and effectively in a Roman. True, but the fact is he did not. And it is with that fact that we must deal.

The second important fact for our consideration is that Jesus was a poor Jew. There is recorded in Luke the account of the dedication of Jesus at the temple: "And when the days of her purification according to the law of Moses were accomplished, they brought him . . . to the Lord; (as it is written in the law of the Lord, Every male that openeth the womb shall be called holy to the Lord;) and to offer a sacrifice according to that which is said in the law of the Lord, A pair of turtledoves, or two young pigeons." When we examine the regulation in Leviticus, an interesting fact is revealed: "And when the days of her purifying are fulfilled, for a son, . . . she shall bring a lamb of the first year for a burnt offering, and a young pigeon, or a turtledove, for a sin offering. . . . And if she be not able to bring a lamb, then she shall bring two turtles, or two young pigeons; the one for a burnt offering and the other for a sin offering." It is clear from the text that the mother of Jesus was one whose means were not sufficient for a lamb, and who was compelled, therefore, to use doves or young pigeons.

The economic predicament with which he was identified in birth placed him initially with the great mass of men on the earth. The masses of the people are poor. If we dare take the position that in Jesus there was at work some radical destiny, it would be safe to say that in his poverty he was more truly Son of man than he would have been if the incident of family or birth had made him a rich son of

17

Israel. It is not a point to be labored, for again and again men have transcended circumstance of birth and training; but it is an observation not without merit.

The third fact is that Jesus was a member of a minority group in the midst of a larger dominant and controlling group. In 63 B.C. Palestine fell into the hands of the Romans. After this date the gruesome details of loss of status were etched, line by line, in the sensitive soul of Israel, dramatized ever by an increasing desecration of the Holy Land. To be sure, there was Herod, an Israelite, who ruled from 37 to 4 B.C.; but in some ways he was completely apostate. Taxes of all kinds increased, and out of these funds, extracted from the vitals of the people, temples in honor of Emperor Augustus were built within the boundaries of the holy soil. It was a sad and desolate time for the people. Herod became the symbol of shame and humiliation for all of Israel.

In Galilee a certain revolutionary, whose name was Judas, laid siege to the armory at Sepphoris and, with weapons taken there, tried to re-establish the political glory of Israel. How terrible a moment! The whole city of Sepphoris was regarded as a hostage, and Roman soldiers, aided by the warriors of King Aretas of Arabia, reduced the place to whited ash. In time the city was rebuilt—and perhaps Jesus was one of the carpenters employed from Nazareth, which was a neighboring village.

It is utterly fantastic to assume that Jesus grew to manhood untouched by the surging currents of the common life that made up the climate of Palestine. Not only must he have been aware of them; that he was affected by them is a most natural observation. A word of caution is urgent at this point. To place Jesus against the background of his time is by no means sufficient to explain him. Who can explain a spiritual genius—or any kind of genius, for that matter? The historical setting in which Jesus grew up, the psychological mood and temper of the age and of the House of Israel, the economic and social predicament of Jesus' family—all these are important. But they in themselves are unable to tell us precisely the thing that we most want to know: Why does he differ from many others in the same setting? Any explanation of Jesus in terms of psychology, politics, economics, religion, or the like must inevitably explain his contemporaries as well. It may tell why Jesus was a particular kind of Jew, but not why some other Jews were not Jesus. And that is, after all, the most important question, since the thing which makes him most significant is not the way in which he resembled his fellows but the way in which he differed from all the rest of them. Jesus inherited the same traits as countless other Jews of his . time; he grew up in the same society; and yet he was Jesus, and the others were not. Uniqueness always escapes us as we undertake an analysis of character.

On the other hand, these considerations should not blind us to the significance of the environmental factors and the social and religious heritage of Jesus in determining the revolutionary character of some of his insights. One of the clearest and simplest statements of the issues here raised, and their bearing upon the character and teaching of Jesus, is found in Vladimir Simkhovitch's *Toward the Under-standing of Jesus.* I am using his essay as the basis for our discussion of the problem, but the applications are mine. Simkhovitch says:

In the year 6 Judea was annexed to Syria; in the year 70 Jerusalem and its temple were destroyed. Between these two dates Jesus preached and was crucified on Golgotha. During all that time the life of the little nation was a terrific drama; its patriotic emotions were aroused to the highest pitch and then still more inflamed by the identification of national politics with a national religion. Is it reasonable to assume that what was going on before Jesus' eyes was a closed book, that the ago-nizing problems of his people were a matter of indifference to him, that he had given them no consideration, that he was not taking a definite attitude towards the great and all-absorbing problem of the very people whom he taught? [2]

There is one overmastering problem that the socially and politically disinherited always face: Under what terms is survival possible? In the case of the Jewish people in the Greco-Roman world the problem was even more acute than under ordinary circumstances, because it had to do not only with physical survival in terms of life and limb but also with the actual survival of a culture and a faith. Juda-ism was a culture, a civilization, and a religion—a total world view in which there was no provision for any form of thoroughgoing dualism. The crucial problem of Judaism was to exist as an isolated, autonomous, cultural, religious, and political unit in the midst of the hostile Hellenic world.

If there had been sharp lines distinguishing the culture from the religion, or the religion from political autonomy, a compromise could have been worked out. Because the Jews thought that a basic compromise was possible, they sought political annexation to Syria which would bring them under Roman rule directly and thereby guarantee them, within the framework of Roman policy, religious and cultural autonomy. But this merely aggravated the already tense nationalistic feeling and made a direct, all-out attack against Roman authority inevitable.

In the midst of this psychological climate Jesus began his teaching and his ministry. His words were directed to the House of Israel, a minority within the Greco-Roman world, smarting under the loss of status, freedom, and autonomy, haunted by the dream of the restoration of a lost glory and a former greatness. His message focused on the urgency of a radical change in the inner attitude of the people. He recognized fully that out of the heart are the issues of life and that no external force, however great and overwhelming, can at long last destroy a people if it does not first win the victory of the spirit against them. "To revile because one has been reviled—this is the real evil because it is the evil of the soul itself." Jesus saw this with almighty clarity. Again and again he came back to the inner life of the individual. With increasing insight and startling accuracy he placed his finger on the "inward center" as the crucial arena where the issues would determine the destiny of his people.

When I was a seminary student, I attended one of the

great quadrennial conventions of the Student Volunteer Movement. One afternoon some seven hundred of us had a special group meeting, at which a Korean girl was asked to talk to us about her impression of American education. It was an occasion to be remembered. The Korean student was very personable and somewhat diminutive. She came to the edge of the platform and, with what seemed to be obvious emotional strain, she said, "You have asked me to talk with you about my impression of American education. But there is only one thing that a Korean has any right to talk about, and that is freedom from Japan." For about twenty minutes she made an impassioned plea for the freedom of her people, ending her speech with this sentence: "If you see a little American boy and you ask him what he wants, he says, 'I want a penny to put in my bank or to buy a whistle or a piece of candy.' But if you see a little Korean boy and you ask him what he wants, he says, 'I want freedom from Japan.' "

It was this kind of atmosphere that characterized the life of the Jewish community when Jesus was a youth in Palestine. The urgent question was what must be the attitude toward Rome. Was any attitude possible that would be morally tolerable and at the same time preserve a basic self-esteem—without which life could not possibly have any meaning? The question was not academic. It was the most crucial of questions. In essence, Rome was the enemy; Rome symbolized total frustration; Rome was the great barrier to peace of mind. And Rome was everywhere. No Jewish person of the period could deal with the question of his practical life, his vocation, his place in society, until first he had settled deep within himself this critical issue.

This is the position of the disinherited in every age. What must be the attitude toward the rulers, the controllers of political, social, and economic life? This is the question of the Negro in American life. Until he has faced and settled that question, he cannot inform his environment with reference to his own life, whatever may be his preparation or his pretensions.

In the main, there were two alternatives faced by the Jewish minority of which Jesus was a part. Simply stated, these were to resist or not to resist. But each of these alternatives has within it secondary alternatives.

Under the general plan of nonresistance one may take the position of imitation. The aim of such an attitude is to assimilate the culture and the social behavior-pattern of the dominant group. It is the profound capitulation to the powerful, because it means the yielding of oneself to that which, deep within, one recognizes as being unworthy. It makes for a strategic loss of self-respect. The aim is to reduce all outer or external signs of difference to zero, so that there shall be no ostensible cause for active violence or opposition. Under some circumstances it may involve a repudiation of one's heritage, one's customs, one's faith. Accurate imitation until the façade of complete assimilation is securely placed and the antagonism of difference dissolved—such is the function of this secondary alternative within the broader alternative of nonresistance. Herod was an excellent example of this solution.

23

To some extent this was also the attitude of the Sadducees. They represented the "upper" class. From their number came the high priests, and most of the economic security derived from contemporary worship in the temple was their monopoly. They did not represent the masses of the people. Any disturbance of the established order meant upsetting their position. They loved Israel, but they seem to have loved security more. They made their public peace with Rome and went on about the business of living. They were astute enough to see that their own position could be perpetuated if they stood firmly against all revolutionaries and radicals. Such persons would only stir the people to resist the inevitable, and in the end everything would be lost. Their tragedy was in the fact that they idealized the position of the Roman in the world and suffered the moral fate of the Romans by becoming like them. They saw only two roads open before them—become like the Romans or be destroyed by the Romans. They chose the former.

The other alternative in the nonresistance pattern is to reduce contact with the enemy to a minimum. It is the attitude of cultural isolation in the midst of a rejected culture. Cunning the mood may be—one of bitterness and hatred, but also one of deep, calculating fear. To take up active resistance would be foolhardy, for a thousand reasons. The only way out is to keep one's resentment under rigid control and censorship.

The issue raised by this attitude is always present. The opposition to those who work for social change does not

imitation vs. rejection

come only from those who are the guarantors of the *status quo*. Again and again it has been demonstrated that the lines are held by those whose hold on security is sure only as long as the *status quo* remains intact. The reasons for this are not far to seek. If a man is convinced that he is safe only as long as he uses his power to give others a sense of insecurity, then the measure of their security is in his hands. If security or insecurity is at the mercy of a single individual or group, then control of behavior becomes routine. All imperialism functions in this way. Subject peoples are held under control by this device.

One of the most striking scenes in the movie *Ben Hur* was that in which a Roman legion marches by while hundreds of people stand silently on the roadside. As the last soldier passes, a very dignified, self-possessed Jewish gentleman, with folded arms and eyes smoldering with the utmost contempt, without the slightest shift of his facial muscles spits at the heel of the receding legionary—a consummate touch. Such—in part, at least—was the attitude of the Pharisee. No active resistance against Rome—only a terrible contempt. Obviously such an attitude is a powder keg. One nameless incident may cause to burst into flame the whole gamut of smoldering passion, leaving nothing in its wake but charred corpses, mute reminders of the tragedy of life. Jesus saw this and understood it clearly.

The other major alternative is resistance. It may be argued that even nonresistance is a form of resistance, for it may be regarded as an appositive dimension of resistance. Resistance may be overt action, or it may be merely mental and moral attitudes. For the purposes of our discussion resistance is defined as the physical, overt expression of an inner attitude. Resistance in this sense finds its most dramatic manifestation in force of arms.

Armed resistance is apt to be a tragic last resort in the life of the disinherited. Armed resistance has an appeal because it provides a form of expression, of activity, that releases tension and frees the oppressed from a disintegrating sense of complete impotency and helplessness. "Why can't we do something? Something must be done!" is the recurring cry. By "something" is meant action, direct action, as over against words, subtleties, threats, and innuendoes. It is better to die fighting for freedom than to rot away in one's chains, the argument runs.

> Before I'd be a slave
> I'd be buried in my grave,
> And go home to my God
> And be free!

The longer the mood is contemplated, the more insistent the appeal. It is a form of fanaticism, to be sure, but that may not be a vote against it. In all action there is operative a fringe of irrationality. Once the mood is thoroughly established, any council of caution is interpreted as either compromise or cowardice. The fact that the ruler has available to him the power of the state and complete access to all arms is scarcely considered. Out of the deeps of the heart there swells a great and awful assurance that because the cause is just, it cannot fail. Any failure is regarded as temporary and, to the devoted, as a testing of character.

This was the attitude of the Zealots of Jesus' day. There was added appeal in their position because it called forth from the enemy organized determination and power. It is never to be forgotten that one of the ways by which men measure their own significance is to be found in the amount of power and energy other men must use in order to crush them or hold them back. This is at least one explanation of the fact that even a weak and apparently inconsequential movement becomes formidable under the pressure of great persecution. The persecution becomes a vote of confidence, which becomes, in turn, a source of inspiration, power, and validation. The Zealots knew this. Jesus knew this. It is a matter of more than passing significance that he had a Zealot among his little band of followers, indeed among the twelve chosen ones.

In the face of these alternatives Jesus came forth with still another. On this point Simkhovitch makes a profound contribution to the understanding of the psychology of Jesus. He reminds us that Jesus expressed his alternative in a "brief formula—The Kingdom of Heaven is in us." He states further:

Jesus had to resent deeply the loss of Jewish national independence and the aggression of Rome. . . . Natural humiliation was hurting and burning. The balm for that burning humiliation was humility. For humility cannot be humiliated. . . . Thus he asked his people to learn from him, "For I am

27

meek and lowly in heart; and ye shall find rest unto your souls. For my yoke is easy, and my burden is light." [3]

It was but natural that such a position would be deeply resented by many of his fellows, who were suffering even as he was. To them it was a complete betrayal to the enemy. It was to them a counsel of acquiescence, if not of despair, full to overflowing with a kind of groveling and stark cowardice. Besides, it seemed like self-deception, like whistling in the dark. All of this would have been quite true if Jesus had stopped there. He did not. He recognized with authentic realism that anyone who permits another to determine the quality of his inner life gives into the hands of the other the keys to his destiny. If a man knows precisely what he can do to you or what epithet he can hurl against you in order to make you lose your temper, your equilibrium, then he can always keep you under subjection. It is a man's reaction to things that determines their ability to exercise power over him. It seems clear that Jesus understood the anatomy of the relationship between his people and the Romans, and he interpreted that relationship against the background of the profoundest ethical insight of his own religious faith as he had found it in the heart of the prophets of Israel.

The solution which Jesus found for himself and for Israel, as they faced the hostility of the Greco-Roman world, becomes the word and the work of redemption for all the cast-down people in every generation and in every

[3] *Toward the Understanding of Jesus,* pp. 60-61. Copyright 1921, 1937, 1947 by The Macmillan Co. and used with their permission.

28

age. I mean this quite literally. I do not ignore the theological and metaphysical interpretation of the Christian doctrine of salvation. But the underprivileged everywhere have long since abandoned any hope that this type of salvation deals with the crucial issues by which their days are turned into despair without consolation. The basic fact is that Christianity as it was born in the mind of this Jewish teacher and thinker appears as a technique of survival for the oppressed. That it became, through the intervening years, a religion of the powerful and the dominant, used sometimes as an instrument of oppression, must not tempt us into believing that it was thus in the mind and life of Jesus. "In him was life; and the life was the light of men." Wherever his spirit appears, the oppressed gather fresh courage; for he announced the good news that fear, hypocrisy, and hatred, the three hounds of hell that track the trail of the disinherited, need have no dominion over them.

I belong to a generation that finds very little that is meaningful or intelligent in the teachings of the Church concerning Jesus Christ. It is a generation largely in revolt because of the general impression that Christianity is essentially an other-worldly religion, having as its motto: "Take all the world, but give me Jesus." The desperate opposition to Christianity rests in the fact that it seems, in the last analysis, to be a betrayal of the Negro into the hands of his enemies by focusing his attention upon heaven, forgiveness, love, and the like. It is true that this emphasis is germane to the religion of Jesus, but it has to be put into a context that will show its strength and vitality rather than its weakness and failure. For years it has been a part of my own quest so to understand the religion of Jesus that interest in his way of life could be developed and sustained by intelligent men and women who were at the same time deeply victimized by the Christian Church's betrayal of his faith.

During much of my boyhood I was cared for by my grandmother, who was born a slave and lived until the Civil War on a plantation near Madison, Florida. My regular chore was to do all of the reading for my grandmother—she could neither read nor write. Two or three times a week I read the Bible aloud to her. I was deeply impressed by the fact that she was most particular about the choice of Scripture. For instance, I might read many of the more devotional Psalms, some of Isaiah, the Gospels again and again. But the Pauline epistles, never—except, at long intervals, the thirteenth chapter of First Corinthians. My curiosity knew no bounds, but we did not question her about anything.

When I was older and was half through college, I chanced to be spending a few days at home near the end of summer vacation. With a feeling of great temerity I asked her one day why it was that she would not let me read any of the Pauline letters. What she told me I shall never forget. "During the days of slavery," she said, "the master's minister would occasionally hold services for the slaves. Old man McGhee was so mean that he would not let a Negro minister preach to his slaves. Always the white minister used as his text something from Paul. At least three or four times a year he used as a text: 'Slaves, be obedient to them that are your masters . . . , as unto Christ.' Then he would go on to show how it was God's will that we were slaves and how, if we were good and happy slaves, God would bless us. I promised my Maker that if I ever learned to read and if freedom ever came, I would not read that part of the Bible."

Since that fateful day on the front porch in Florida I have been working on the problem her words presented. A part of the fruits of that search throw an important light upon the issues with which I am dealing. It cannot be denied that too often the weight of the Christian movement has been on the side of the strong and the powerful and against the weak and oppressed—this, despite the gospel. A part of the responsibility seems to me to rest upon a peculiar twist in the psychology of Paul, whose wide and universal concern certainly included all men, bond and free.

Let us examine the facts. The apostle Paul was a Jew. He was the first great creative interpreter of Christianity. His letters are older than the Gospels themselves. It seems that because he was not one of the original disciples, he was never quite accepted by them as one able to speak with authority concerning the Master. This fact hung very heavily upon the soul of the apostle. He did not ever belong, quite. One of the disciples could always say, "But of course you do not quite understand, because, you see, you were not there when . . ."

But the fact remains: Paul was a Jew, even as Jesus was a Jew. By blood, training, background, and religion he be-

31

longed to the Jewish minority, about whom we have been speaking. But unlike them, for the most part, he was a free Jew; he was a citizen of Rome. A desert and a sea were placed between his status in the empire and that of his fellow Jews. A very searching dilemma was created by this fact. On the one hand, he belonged to the privileged class. He had the freedom of the empire at his disposal. There were certain citizenship rights which he could claim despite his heritage, faith, and religion. Should he deny himself merely because he was more fortunate than his fellows? To what extent could he accept his rights without feeling a deep sense of guilt and betrayal? He was of a minority but with majority privileges. If a Roman soldier in some prison in Asia Minor was taking advantage of him, he could make an appeal directly to Caesar. There was always available to him a protection guaranteed by the state and respected by the minions of the state. It was like a magic formula always available in emergencies. It is to the credit of the amazing power of Jesus Christ over the life of Paul that there is only one recorded instance in which he used his privilege.

It is quite understandable that his sense of security would influence certain aspects of his philosophy of history. Naturally he would have a regard for the state, for the civil magistrate, unlike that of his fellows, who regarded them as the formal expression of legitimatized intolerance. The stability of Paul's position in the state was guaranteed by the integrity of the state. One is not surprised, then, to hear him tell slaves to obey their masters like Christ, and say all government is ordained of God. (It is not to meet the argument to say that in a sense everything that is, is permitted of God, or that government and rulers are sustained by God as a concession to the frailty of man.) It would be grossly misleading and inaccurate to say that there are not to be found in the Pauline letters utterances of a deeply different quality—utterances which reveal how his conception transcended all barriers of race and class and condition. But this other side is there, always available to those who wish to use the weight of the Christian message to oppress and humiliate their fellows. The point is that this aspect of Paul's teaching is understandable against the background of his Roman citizenship. It influenced his philosophy of history and resulted in a major frustration that has borne bitter fruit in the history of the movement which he, Paul, did so much to project on the conscience of the human race.

Now Jesus was not a Roman citizen. He was not protected by the normal guarantees of citizenship—that quiet sense of security which comes from knowing that you belong and the general climate of confidence which it inspires. If a Roman soldier pushed Jesus into a ditch, he could not appeal to Caesar; he would be just another Jew in the ditch. Standing always beyond the reach of citizen security, he was perpetually exposed to all the "arrows of outrageous fortune," and there was only a gratuitous refuge—if any—within the state. What stark insecurity! What a breeder of complete civil and moral nihilism and psychic anarchy! Unless one actually lives day by day without a sense of security, he cannot understand what worlds separated Jesus from Paul at this point.

The striking similarity between the social position of Jesus in Palestine and that of the vast majority of American Negroes is obvious to anyone who tarries long over the facts. We are dealing here with conditions that produce essentially the same psychology. There is meant no further comparison. It is the similarity of a social climate at the point of a denial of full citizenship which creates the problem for creative survival. For the most part, Negroes assume that there are no basic citizenship rights, no fundamental protection, guaranteed to them by the state, because their status as citizens has never been clearly defined. There has been for them little protection from the dominant controllers of society and even less protection from the unrestrained elements within their own group.

The result has been a tendency to be their own protectors, to bulwark themselves against careless and deliberate aggression. The Negro has felt, with some justification, that the peace officer of the community provides no defense against the offending or offensive white man; and for an entirely different set of reasons the peace officer gives no protection against the offending Negro. Thus the Negro feels that he must be prepared, at a moment's notice, to protect his own life and take the consequence therefor. Such a predicament has made it natural for some of them to use weapons as a defense and to have recourse to premeditated or precipitate violence.

Living in a climate of deep insecurity, Jesus, faced with

so narrow a margin of civil guarantees, had to find some other basis upon which to establish a sense of well-being. He knew that the goals of religion as he understood them could never be worked out within the then-established order. Deep from within that order he projected a dream, the logic of which would give to all the needful security. There would be room for all, and no man would be a threat to his brother. "The kingdom of God is within." "The Spirit of the Lord is upon me, because he hath anointed me to preach the gospel to the poor."

The basic principles of his way of life cut straight through to the despair of his fellows and found it groundless. By inference he says, "You must abandon your fear of each other and fear only God. You must not indulge in any deception and dishonesty, even to save your lives. Your words must be Yea—Nay; anything else is evil. Hatred is destructive to hated and hater alike. Love your enemy, that you may be children of your Father who is in heaven."

CHAPTER TWO

Fear

FEAR is one of the persistent hounds of hell that dog the footsteps of the poor, the dispossessed, the disinherited. There is nothing new or recent about fear—it is doubtless as old as the life of man on the planet. Fears are of many kinds—fear of objects, fear of people, fear of the future, fear of nature, fear of the unknown, fear of old age, fear of disease, and fear of life itself. Then there is fear which has to do with aspects of experience and detailed states of mind. Our homes, institutions, prisons, churches, are crowded with people who are hounded by day and harrowed by night because of some fear that lurks ready to spring into action as soon as one is alone, or as soon as the lights go out, or as soon as one's social defenses are temporarily removed.

The ever-present fear that besets the vast poor, the economically and socially insecure, is a fear of still a different breed. It is a climate closing in; it is like the fog in San Francisco or in London. It is nowhere in particular yet everywhere. It is a mood which one carries around with himself, distilled from the acrid conflict with which his days are surrounded. It has its roots deep in the heart of the relations between the weak and the strong, between the controllers of environment and those who are controlled by it.

When the basis of such fear is analyzed, it is clear that it arises out of the sense of isolation and helplessness in the face of the varied dimensions of violence to which the underprivileged are exposed. Violence, precipitate and stark, is the sire of the fear of such people. It is spawned by the perpetual threat of violence everywhere. Of course, physical violence is the most obvious cause. But here, it is important to point out, a particular kind of physical violence or its counterpart is evidenced; it is violence that is devoid of the element of contest. It is what is feared by the rabbit that cannot ultimately escape the hounds. One can almost see the desperation creep into the quivering, pulsing body of the frightened animal. It is one-sided violence. If two men equally matched, or even relatively matched, are in deadly combat, the violence is clear-cut though terrible; there is gross equality of advantage. But when the power and the tools of violence are on one side, the fact that there is no available and recognized protection from violence makes the resulting fear deeply terrifying.

In a society in which certain people or groups—by virtue of economic, social, or political power—have dead-weight advantages over others who are essentially without that kind of power, those who are thus disadvantaged know that they cannot fight back effectively, that they cannot protect themselves, and that they cannot demand protection from their persecutors. Any slight conflict, any alleged insult, any vague whim, any unrelated frustration, may bring down upon the head of the defenseless the full weight of naked physical violence. Even in such a circumstance it is not the fear of death that is most often at work; it is the deep humiliation arising from dying without benefit of cause or purpose. No high end is served. There is no trumpet blast to stir the blood and to anesthetize the agony. Here there is no going down to the grave with a shout; it is merely being killed or being beaten in utter wrath or indifferent sadism, without the dignity of being on the receiving end of a premeditated act hammered out in the white heat of a transcendent moral passion. The whole experience attacks the fundamental sense of self-respect and personal dignity, without which a man is no man.

In such physical violence the contemptuous disregard for personhood is the fact that is degrading. If a man knows that he is the object of deliberately organized violence, in which care has been exercised to secure the most powerful and deadly weapon in order to destroy him, there may be something great and stimulating about his end. Conceivably this is a lesson that may be learned from one interpretation of the slaying of the giant Goliath. The great Goliath, the symbol of the might and prowess of the Philistines, is equipped for battle, armor replete, sword and protectors in order. Then there is David, just a lad—perhaps in short shirt, possibly without even sandals. For him no armor, no sword, no helmet—just a boy with a slingshot in his hand. David's preparation for battle may be thought to reflect David's estimate of the might and prowess of the Philistines. When the great Goliath beheld David, and the full weight of the drama broke upon him with force, it well might be literally true that under the tension growing out of a sense of outraged dignity he burst a blood vessel, resulting in apoplexy.

Always back of the threat is the rumor or the fact that somewhere, under some similar circumstances violence was used. That is all that is necessary. The threat becomes the effective instrument. There was a dog that lived at the end of my street in my home town. Every afternoon he came down the street by the house. I could always hear him coming, giving a quick, sharp yelp in front of certain yards along the way. He was not hit by flying stones; each boy would catch the dog's eye and draw his arm back—the yelp followed immediately. The threat was sufficient to secure the reaction because, somewhere in the past, that particular motion had been identified with pain and injury. Such is the role of the threat of violence. It is rooted in a past experience, actual or reported, which tends to guarantee the present reaction of fear.

The disinherited experience the disintegrating effect of contempt in some such fashion as did Goliath. There are few things more devastating than to have it burned into you that you do not count and that no provisions are made for the literal protection of your person. The threat of violence is ever present, and there is no way to determine precisely when it may come crushing down upon you. In modern power politics this is called a war of nerves. The underprivileged in any society are the victims of a perpetual war of nerves. The logic of the state of affairs is physical violence, but it need not fulfill itself in order to work its perfect havoc in the souls of the poor.

Fear, then, becomes the safety device with which the oppressed surround themselves in order to give some measure of protection from complete nervous collapse. How do they achieve this? In the first place, they make their bodies commit to memory ways of behaving that will tend to reduce their exposure to violence. Several years ago, when I was in India, I experienced precisely what is meant here. It was on our first evening in the country that a friend came to visit and to give advice about certain precautions to be observed. Just before he left, a final caution was given about snakes. He advised that we should not walk around at night without a light, not go into an unlighted room at night. We should sleep with a flashlight under the pillow, so that if it were necessary to get up during the night, a circle of light could be thrown on the floor before stepping out of bed, lest we disturb the nocturnal rambling of some unsuspecting cobra. I sat alone for some time after he left. During that period of concentration I was literally teaching my body how to behave, so that after that particular evening it would be extremely difficult for me to violate his expressed advice. My conditioning was so complete that, subsequently, my behavior was automatic.

This is precisely what the weak do everywhere. Through

bitter experience they have learned how to exercise extreme care, how to behave so as to reduce the threat of immediate danger from their environment. Fear thus becomes a form of life assurance, making possible the continuation of physical existence with a minimum of active violence.

Children are taught how to behave in this same way. The children of the disinherited live a restricted childhood. From their earliest moments they are conditioned so as to reduce their exposure to violence. In Felix Salten's *Bambi*, the old stag counsels Bambi, giving to him in great detail a pattern of behavior that will reduce his chance of being shot without an opportunity for escape. He teaches him to distinguish human scent, the kinds of exposure that may be deadly, what precise kind of behavior is relatively safe. The stag is unwilling to leave Bambi until he is sure that the young deer has made his body commit to memory ways of behaving that will protect and safeguard his life.

The threat of violence within a framework of well-nigh limitless power is a weapon by which the weak are held in check. Artificial limitations are placed upon them, restricting freedom of movement, of employment, and of participation in the common life. These limitations are given formal or informal expression in general or specific policies of separateness or segregation. These policies tend to freeze the social status of the insecure. The threat of violence may be implemented not only by constituted authority but also by anyone acting in behalf of the established order. Every member of the controllers' group is in a sense a special deputy, authorized by the mores to enforce the pattern.

This fact tends to create fear, which works on behalf of the proscriptions and guarantees them. The anticipation of possible violence makes it very difficult for any escape from the pattern to be effective.

It is important to analyze the functioning of segregation that we may better understand the nature of the fear it engenders. It is obvious that segregation can be established only between two groups that are unequal in power and control. Two groups that are relatively equal in power in a society may enter into a voluntary arrangement of separateness. Segregation can apply only to a relationship involving the weak and the strong. For it means that limitations are arbitrarily set up, which, in the course of time, tend to become fixed and to seem normal in governing the etiquette between the two groups. A peculiar characteristic of segregation is the ability of the stronger to shuttle back and forth between the prescribed areas with complete immunity and a kind of mutually tacit sanction; while the position of the weaker, on the other hand, is quite definitely fixed and frozen.

A very simple illustration is the operation of Jim Crow travel in trains in the southern part of the United States. On such a train the porter, when he is not in line of duty, may ride only in the Jim Crow coach—for the train porter is a Negro. But the members of the train crew who are not Negroes—the conductor, brakeman, baggageman—when they are not working, may ride either in the Jim Crow section or in any other section of the train. In the town in Florida in which I grew up as a boy it was a common occurrence for white persons to attend our church services and share in the worship. But it was quite impossible for any of us to do the same in the white churches of the community. All over the world, wherever ghettos are found, the same basic elements appear—a fact which dramatizes the position of weakness and gives the widest possible range to the policing effect of fear generated by the threat of violence.

Given segregation as a factor determining relations, the resources of the environment are made into instruments to enforce the artificial position. Most of the accepted social behavior-patterns assume segregation to be normal—if normal, then correct; if correct, then moral; if moral, then religious. Religion is thus made a defender and guarantor of the presumptions. God, for all practical purposes, is imaged as an elderly, benign white man, seated on a white throne, with bright, white light emanating from his countenance. Angels are blonds and brunets suspended in the air around his throne to be his messengers and execute his purposes. Satan is viewed as being red with the glow of fire. But the imps, the messengers of the devil, are black. The phrase "black as an imp" is a stereotype.

The implications of such a view are simply fantastic in the intensity of their tragedy. Doomed on earth to a fixed and unremitting status of inferiority, of which segregation is symbolic, and at the same time cut off from the hope that the Creator intended it otherwise, those who are thus victimized are stripped of all social protection. It is vicious and thoroughly despicable to rationalize this position, the product of a fear that is as sordid as it is unscrupulous, into acceptance. Under such circumstances there is but a step from being despised to despising oneself.

The fear that segregation inspires among the weak in turn breeds fear among the strong and the dominant. This fear insulates the conscience against a sense of wrongdoing in carrying out a policy of segregation. For it counsels that if there were no segregation, there would be no protection against invasion of the home, the church, the school. This fear perpetuates the Jewish ghettos in Western civilization, the restrictive covenants in California and other states, the Chinatowns, the Little Tokyos, and the Street of the Untouchables in Hindu lands.[1]

The Jewish community has long been acquainted with segregation and the persecution growing out of it. Jews have been all the more easily trapped by it because of the deep historical conviction that they are a chosen people. This conviction and its underscoring in the unique ethical insights of the prophets have tended to make all those who were not a part of Israel feel in some sense as if they were spiritual outcasts. The conscious and unconscious reaction inspired by this sense of being on the outside is a fertile seedbed for anti-Semitism. Anti-Semitism is a confession of a deep sense of inferiority and moral insecurity. It is the fear of the socially or politically strong in the presence of the threat of moral judgment implicit in the role of the

[1] Recently untouchability was outlawed by the Indian state. A Hindu government did what years of British rule failed to do. Perhaps this is as it should be.

Jewish community throughout human history. Jesus was intimately acquainted with this problem from the inside. Jesus knew all of this.

> His days were nurtured in great hostilities
> Focused upon his kind, the sons of Israel.
> There was no moment in all his years
> When he was free.[2]

It is instructive to inquire into the effects of fear on the disadvantaged. Fear becomes acute, in the form of panic or rage, only at the moment when what has been threat becomes actual violence; but the mere anticipation of such an encounter is overwhelming simply because the odds are basically uneven. This fact is important to hold in mind. The disadvantaged man knows that in any conflict he must deal not only with the particular individual involved but also with the entire group, then or later. Even recourse to the arbitration of law tends to be avoided because of the fear that the interpretations of law will be biased on the side of the dominant group. The result is the dodging of all encounters. The effect is nothing short of disaster in the organism; for, studies show, fear actually causes chemical changes in the body, affecting the blood stream and the muscular reactions, preparing the body either for fight or for flight. If flight is resorted to, it merely serves as an incentive to one's opponent to track down and overpower.

[2] From my privately published volume of poems, *The Greatest of These*, p. 3.

Furthermore, not to fight back at the moment of descending violence is to be a coward, and to be deeply and profoundly humiliated in one's own estimation and in that of one's friends and family. If he is a man, he stands in the presence of his woman as not a man. While it may be true that many have not had such experiences, yet each stands in candidacy for such an experience.

→ It is clear, then, that this fear, which served originally as a safety device, a kind of protective mechanism for the weak, finally becomes death for the self. The power that saves turns executioner. Within the walls of separateness death keeps watch. There are some who defer this death by yielding all claim to personal significance beyond the little world in which they live. In the absence of all hope ambition dies, and the very self is weakened, corroded. There remains only the elemental will to live and to accept life on the terms that are available. There is a profound measure of resourcefulness in all life, a resourcefulness that is guaranteed by the underlying aliveness of life itself.

The crucial question, then, is this: Is there any help to be found in the religion of Jesus that can be of value here? It is utterly beside the point to examine here what the religion of Jesus suggests to those who would be helpful to the disinherited. That is ever in the nature of special pleading. No man wants to be the object of his fellow's pity. Obviously, if the strong put forth a great redemptive effort to change the social, political, and economic arrangements in which they seem to find their basic security, the

46

whole picture would be altered. But this is apart from my thesis. Again the crucial question: Is there any help to be found for the disinherited in the religion of Jesus?

Did Jesus deal with this kind of fear? If so, how did he do it? It is not merely, What did he say? even though his words are the important clues available to us.

An analysis of the teaching of Jesus reveals that there is much that deals with the problems created by fear. After his temptation in the wilderness Jesus appeared in the synagogue and was asked to read the lesson. He chose to read from the prophet Isaiah the words which he declared as his fulfillment:

> The Spirit of the Lord is upon me,
> because he hath anointed me . . .
> to preach deliverance to the captives,
> and recovering of sight to the blind,
> to set at liberty them that are bruised,
> to preach the acceptable year of the Lord.

And he closed the book. . . . And he began to say unto them, This day is this scripture fulfilled in your ears.

In the Song of Mary we find words which anticipate the same declaration of Jesus:

> He hath scattered the proud in the imagination of their hearts.
> He hath put down the mighty from their seats,
> and exalted them of low degree.
> He hath filled the hungry with good things;
> and the rich he hath sent empty away.

47

The most specific statement which Jesus makes dealing with the crux of the problem is found in the tenth chapter of Matthew:

Fear them not therefore: for there is nothing covered, that shall not be revealed; and hid, that shall not be known. . . . And fear not them which kill the body, but are not able to kill the soul: but rather fear him which is able to destroy both soul and body in hell. Are not two sparrows sold for a farthing? and one of them shall not fall on the ground without your Father. But the very hairs of your head are all numbered. Fear ye not therefore, ye are of more value than many sparrows.

Again in Luke:

Fear not, little flock; for it is your Father's good pleasure to give you the kingdom.

In the great expression of affirmation and faith found in the Sermon on the Mount there appears in clearest outline the basis of his positive answer to the awful fact of fear and its twin sons of thunder—anxiety and despair:

Therefore I say unto you, Take no thought for your life, what ye shall eat, or what ye shall drink; nor yet for your body, what ye shall put on. Is not the life more than meat, and the body than raiment? Behold the fowls of the air: for they sow not, neither do they reap, nor gather into barns; yet your heavenly Father feedeth them. Are ye not much better than they? Which of you by taking thought can add one cubit unto his stature? And why take ye thought for raiment? Consider the lilies of the field, how they grow; they toil not, neither do they spin: And yet I say unto you, That even Solomon in all his glory was not arrayed like one of these. Wherefore, if God so clothe the grass of the field, which to day is, and to morrow is cast into the oven, shall he not much more clothe you, O ye of little faith? Therefore take no thought, saying, What shall we eat? or, What shall we drink? or, Wherewithal shall we be clothed? (For after all these things do the Gentiles seek:) for your heavenly Father knoweth that ye have need of all these things. But seek ye first the kingdom of God, and his righteousness; and all these things shall be added unto you. Take therefore no thought for the morrow: for the morrow shall take thought for the things of itself. Sufficient unto the day is the evil thereof.

The core of the analysis of Jesus is that man is a child of God, the God of life that sustains all of nature and guarantees all the intricacies of the life-process itself. Jesus suggests that it is quite unreasonable to assume that God, whose creative activity is expressed even in such details as the hairs of a man's head, would exclude from his concern the life, the vital spirit, of the man himself. This idea—that God is mindful of the individual—is of tremendous import in dealing with fear as a disease. In this world the socially disadvantaged man is constantly given a negative answer to the most important personal questions upon which mental health depends: "Who am I? What am I?" dignity

The first question has to do with a basic self-estimate, a profound sense of belonging, of counting. If a man feels that he does not belong in the way in which it is perfectly normal for other people to belong, then he develops a deep sense of insecurity. When this happens to a person, it provides the basic material for what the psychologist

calls an inferiority complex. It is quite possible for a man
to have no sense of personal inferiority as such, but at the
same time to be dogged by a sense of social inferiority. The
awareness of being a child of God tends to stabilize the
ego and results in a new courage, fearlessness, and power.
I have seen it happen again and again.

When I was a youngster, this was drilled into me by my
grandmother. The idea was given to her by a certain
slave minister who, on occasion, held secret religious meetings with his fellow slaves. How everything in me quivered
with the pulsing tremor of raw energy when, in her recital,
she would come to the triumphant climax of the minister:
"You—you are not niggers. You—you are not slaves. You
are God's children." This established for them the ground
of personal dignity, so that a profound sense of personal
worth could absorb the fear reaction. This alone is not
enough, but without it, nothing else is of value. The first
task is to get the self immunized against the most radical
results of the *threat* of violence. When this is accomplished,
relaxation takes the place of the churning fear. The individual now feels that he counts, that he belongs. He senses
the confirmation of his roots, and even death becomes a
little thing.

All leaders of men have recognized the significance of
this need for a sense of belonging among those who feel
themselves disadvantaged. Several years ago I was talking
with a young German woman who had escaped from the
Nazis; first to Holland, then France, England, and finally
to America. She described for me the powerful magnet

that Hitler was to German youth. The youth had lost their
sense of belonging. They did not count; there was no
center of hope for their marginal egos. According to my
friend, Hitler told them: "No one loves you—I love you;
no one will give you work—I will give you work; no one
wants you—I want you." And when they saw the sunlight
in his eyes, they dropped their tools and followed him. He
stabilized the ego of the German youth, and put it within
their power to overcome their sense of inferiority. It is
true that in the hands of a man like Hitler, power is ex-
ploited and turned to ends which make for havoc and
misery; but this should not cause us to ignore the basic
soundness of the theory upon which he operated.

A man's conviction that he is God's child automatically
tends to shift the basis of his relationship with all his fellows. He recognizes at once that to fear a man, whatever
may be that man's power over him, is a basic denial of
the integrity of his very life. It lifts that mere man to a
place of pre-eminence that belongs to God and to God
alone. He who fears is literally delivered to destruction.
To the child of God, a scale of values becomes available
by which men are measured and their true significance determined. Even the threat of violence, with the possibility
of death that it carries, is recognized for what it is—merely
the threat of violence with a death potential. Such a man
recognizes that death cannot possibly be the worst thing
in the world. There *are* some things that are worse than
death. To deny one's own integrity of personality in the
presence of the human challenge is one of those things.

fear → power to others

"Be not afraid of them that kill the body, and after that have no more that they can do," says Jesus.

One of the practical results following this new orientation is the ability to make an objective, detached appraisal of other people, particularly one's antagonists. Such an appraisal protects one from inaccurate and exaggerated estimations of another person's significance. In a conversation with me Lincoln Steffens once said that he was sure he could rear a child who was a member of a minority group or who was a habitué of a ghetto so as to immunize him against the corroding effects of such limitations.

He said: "I would teach him that he must never call another man 'great'; but that he must always qualify the term with the limiting phrase 'as to,' of the Greek language. A man is never great in general, but he may be great as to something in particular.

"Let me give you an illustration. Once I was the house guest in Berlin of one of the world's greatest scientists. During the first few days of my sojourn, I was completely disorganized. I was nervous, tended to be inarticulate, generally confused, and ill at ease. I had either to get a hold on myself or bring my visit abruptly to an end. One morning while shaving it occurred to me that despite my profound limitations of knowledge in physics and mathematics, I knew infinitely more about politics than did my host. At breakfast I found my tongue and my dignity, and the basis of equality between us was at once restored. My host was a great man *as to* his particular field of natural science, while I was competent in the field of contemporary politics and affairs. This awareness gave me my perspective."

The illustration anticipates the second basic question that must be answered by the disinherited: "What am I?" This question has to do, not with a sense of innate belonging, but rather with personal achievement and ability. All of the inner conflicts and frustrations growing out of limitations of opportunity become dramatically focused here. Even though a man is convinced of his infinite worth as a child of God, this may not in itself give him the opportunity for self-realization and fulfillment that his spirit demands. Even though he may no longer feel himself threatened by violence, the fact remains that for him doors often are closed. There are vocational opportunities that are denied him. It is obvious that the individual must reckon with the external facts of his environment, especially those that constrict his freedom.

There is something more to be said about the inner equipment growing out of the great affirmation of Jesus that a man is a *child* of God. If a man's ego has been stabilized, resulting in a sure grounding of his sense of personal worth and dignity, then he is in a position to appraise his own intrinsic powers, gifts, talents, and abilities. He no longer views his equipment through the darkened lenses of those who are largely responsible for his social predicament. He can think of himself with some measure of detachment from the shackles of his immediate world. If he equips himself in terms of training in this mood, his real ability is brought into play. The fact that he is denied

opportunity will not necessarily deter him. He will post-
pone defeat until defeat itself closes in upon him. The
interesting fact is that defeat may not close in upon him.
Curious indeed is the notion that plays hide-and-seek with
human life: "I may be an exception." A large measure of
illusion and self-deception is implicit in this notion, but
again and again it has come to the rescue of desperate
people forced to take desperate chances.

– The psychological effect on the individual of the conviction that he is a child of God gives a note of integrity
to whatever he does. It provides character in the sense of
sure knowledge and effective performance. After all, this
is what we mean by character when applied to ability in
action. When a man is sick and calls a doctor, what he
wants most to know about the doctor is not the make of
his automobile, or whether he obeys traffic signals, or what
church he attends, or how many children he has, or if he
is married. What is most crucial about the doctor, so far
as the sick man is concerned, is, Can he practice medicine?

Now, what we are discussing has profound bearing upon
the kind of assurance and guidance that should be given
to children who seem destined to develop a sense of defeat
and frustration. The doom of the children is the greatest
tragedy of the disinherited. They are robbed of much of
the careless rapture and spontaneous joy of merely being
alive. Through their environment they are plunged into
the midst of overwhelming pressures for which there can
be no possible preparation. So many tender, joyous things
in them are nipped and killed without their even knowing

the true nature of their loss. The normal for them is the abnormal. Youth is a time of soaring hopes, when dreams are given first wings and, as reconnoitering birds, explore unknown landscapes. Again and again a man full of years is merely the corroboration of the dreams of his youth. The sense of fancy growing out of the sense of fact—which makes all healthy personalities and gives a touch of romance and glory to all of life—first appears as the unrestrained imaginings of youth.

But the child of the disinherited is likely to live a heavy life. A ceiling is placed on his dreaming by the counsel of despair coming from his elders, whom experience has taught to expect little and to hope for less. If, on the other hand, the elders understand in their own experiences and lives the tremendous insight of Jesus, it is possible for them to share their enthusiasm with their children. This is the qualitative overtone springing from the depths of religious insight, and it is contagious. It will put into the hands of the child the key for unlocking the door of his hopes. It must never be forgotten that human beings can be conditioned in favor of the positive as well as the negative. A great and central assurance will cause parents to condition their children to high endeavor and great aspiring, and these in turn will put the child out of the immediate, clawing reaches of the tense or the sustained negations of his environment. I have seen it happen. In communities that were completely barren, with no apparent growing edge, without any point to provide light for the disadvantaged, I have seen children grow up without fear, with quiet dignity and such high purpose that the mark which they set for themselves has even been transcended.

The charge that such thinking is merely rationalizing cannot be made with easy or accepted grace by the man of basic advantage. It ill behooves the man who is not forced to live in a ghetto to tell those who must how to transcend its limitations. The awareness that a man is a child of the God of religion, who is at one and the same time the God of life, creates a profound faith in life that nothing can destroy.

Nothing less than a great daring in the face of overwhelming odds can achieve the inner security in which fear cannot possibly survive. It is true that a man cannot be serene unless he possesses something about which to be serene. Here we reach the high-water mark of prophetic religion, and it is of the essence of the religion of Jesus of Nazareth. Of course God cares for the grass of the field, which lives a day and is no more, or the sparrow that falls unnoticed by the wayside. He also holds the stars in their appointed places, leaves his mark in every living thing. And he cares for me! To be assured of this becomes the answer to the threat of violence—yea, to violence itself. To the degree to which a man knows *this*, he is unconquerable from within and without.

When I was a very small boy, Halley's comet visited our solar system. For a long time I did not see the giant in the sky because I was not permitted to remain up after sundown. My chums had seen it and had told me perfectly amazing things about it. Also I had heard of what were called "comet pills." The theory was that if the pills were taken according to directions, then when the tail of the comet struck the earth one would not be consumed. One night I was awakened by my mother, who told me to dress quickly and come with her out into the backyard to see the comet. I shall never forget it if I live forever. My mother stood with me, her hand resting on my shoulder, while I, in utter, speechless awe, beheld the great spectacle with its fan of light spreading across the heavens. The silence was like that of absolute motion. Finally, after what seemed to me an interminable time interval, I found my speech. With bated breath I said, "What will happen to us if that comet falls out of the sky?"

My mother's silence was so long that I looked from the comet to her face, and there I beheld something in her countenance that I had seen only once before, when I came into her room and found her in prayer. When she spoke, she said, "Nothing will happen to us, Howard; God will take care of us."

O simplehearted mother of mine, in one glorious moment you put your heart on the ultimate affirmation of the human spirit! Many things have I seen since that night. Times without number I have learned that life is hard, as hard as crucible steel; but as the years have unfolded, the majestic power of my mother's glowing words has come back again and again, beating out its rhythmic chant in my own spirit. Here are the faith and the awareness that overcome fear and transform it into the power to strive, to achieve, and not to yield.

CHAPTER THREE

Deception

DECEPTION is perhaps the oldest of all the techniques by which the weak have protected themselves against the strong. Through the ages, at all stages of sentient activity, the weak have survived by fooling the strong.

The techniques of deception seem to be a part of the nervous-reflex action of the organism. The cuttlefish, when attacked, will release some of the fluid from his sepia bag, making the water all around him murky; in the midst of the cloudy water he confuses his attacker and makes his escape. Almost any hunter of birds has seen the mother simulate a broken wing so as to attract attention to herself and thereby save the life of her young. As a boy I have seen the shadow of the hawk on the grassy meadow where I lay resting underneath a shade tree. Consider the behavior of the birds a few feet away as they see the shadow. I have seen them take little feet full of dried grass or leaves, turn an easy half somersault, and play dead. The hawk blinks his eyes, thinks he has had an optical illusion, and goes on to find birds that do not know enough to pretend to be dead. We often played a game of hide-and-seek in which the refrain was, "Lay low, slick duck, the hawk's around." Natural selection has finally resulted in giving to various animals neutral colors or blending colors so that they fade into the landscape and thus protect themselves from destruction by deceiving the enemy.

All little children well know this technique. They know that they cannot cope with the parental will on equal terms. Therefore, in order to carry on their own purposes, they work all kinds of simple—and not so simple—schemes for making the parents do the children's will as if it were their own. Until the teacher catches on, it is a favorite device of students. When a particular lesson has not been studied, or there is danger that the teacher will cover territory that extends beyond the day's preparation, some apparently innocent question is asked about the teacher's prejudice, pet interest, or particular concern. Once the teacher is discussing that particular point, there is nothing more to fear; for before he comes to the end of his talk, the bell will ring and all will be saved.

It is an ancient device that a man-dominated social order has forced upon women, even down to latest times. Olive Schreiner spent much of her energy attacking this form of deception by which the moral life of women was bound. Much of the constant agitation for an equal-rights amendment to the Constitution grows out of recognition of the morally degrading aspects of deception and dishonesty that enter into the relationship between men and women.

When the children of Israel were in captivity in Babylon, the prophet Ezekiel could not give words of comfort and guidance by direct and overt statement. If he had, he would not have lasted very long, and the result would have been a great loss to his people and a tightening of the bonds that held them. He would have been executed as a revolutionary in short order and all religious freedom would have been curtailed. What did the prophet do? He resorted to a form of deception. He put words in the mouth of an old king of Tyre that did not come from him at all, but from Nebuchadrezzar. It was Nebuchadrezzar who had said, "I am a God." He used what we would call now "double talk." But the Jews understood, even though the Babylonian "secret service" was helpless because he was not openly talking against the state.

In a certain southern city a blind Negro had been killed by a policeman. Feeling ran very high. The Negroes were not permitted to have any kind of eulogy or sermon at the funeral service. There was fear of rioting. Nevertheless, the funeral was held, with policemen very much in evidence. There was no sermon, but there was a central prayer. In the prayer the minister told God all that he would have said to the people had he not been under very rigid surveillance. The officers could do nothing, for the minister was not addressing the people; he was talking to his God. How tragically sordid! But it is the old, old method by which the weak have survived through the years.

One of the oldest of the Negro spirituals deals quite

interestingly with this technique. The setting is very dramatic.

The slave had often heard his master's minister talk about heaven, the final abode of the righteous. Naturally the master regarded himself as fitting into the category. On the other hand, the slave knew that he too was going to heaven. He reasoned, "There must be two heavens—no, this cannot be true, because there is only one God. God cannot possibly be divided in this way. I have it! I am having my hell now. When I die, I shall have my heaven. The master's having his heaven now. When he dies, he will have his hell." The next day, chopping cotton beneath the torrid skies, the slave said to his mate:

> I got shoes,
> You got shoes,
> All God's children got shoes.
> When we get to heaven
> We're goin' to put on our shoes
> An' shout all over God's heaven,
> Heaven! Heaven!

Then, looking up to the big house where the master lived, he said:

> Everybody talkin' 'bout heaven
> Ain't goin' there!

Instances could be multiplied from all over the world, and from as far back in human history as records have been kept. It is an old, old defense of the weak against the strong.

The question of deception is not academic, but profoundly ethical and spiritual, going to the very heart of all human relations. For it raises the issue of honesty, integrity, and the consequences thereof over against duplicity and deception and the attendant consequences. Does the fact that a particular course of action jeopardizes a man's life relieve him of the necessity for following that course of action? Are there circumstances under which the ethical question is irrelevant, beside the point? If so, where does one draw the line? Is there a fine distinction between literal honesty and honesty in spirit and intent? Or is truthtelling largely a matter of timing? Are there times when to tell the truth is to be false to the truth that is in you? These questions and many related ones will not be downed. For the disinherited they have to do with the very heart of survival.

It may be argued that a man who places so high a price upon physical existence and survival that he is willing to perjure his own soul has a false, or at least an inadequate, sense of values. "What shall a man give in exchange for his own soul?" Jesus asks. The physical existence of a man makes of him the custodian, the keeper, of the fragment of life which is his. He lives constantly under the necessity to have life fulfill itself. Should he take chances, even in behalf of the values of a kind other than those which have to do with his physical survival? With reference to the question of deception the disinherited are faced with three basic alternatives.

The first alternative is to accept the apparent fact that, one's situation being what it is, there is no sensible choice offered. The individual is disadvantaged because he is not a member of the "party in power," the dominant, controlling group. His word has no value anyway. In any contest he is defeated before he starts. He cannot meet his opponent on equal terms, because there is no basis of equality that exists between the weak and the strong. The only thing that counts is victory—or any level on which victory can be achieved. There can be no question of honesty in dealing with each other, for there is no sense of community. Such a mood takes for granted a facile insincerity.

The fact is, in any great struggle between groups in which the major control of the situation is on one side, the ethical question tends to become merely academic. The advantaged group assumes that they are going to be fooled, if it is possible; there is no expectation of honesty and sincerity. They know that every conceivable device will be used to render ineffective the advantage which they have inherited in their position as the strong. The pattern of deception by which the weak are deprived of their civic, economic, political, and social rights without its appearing that they are so deprived is a matter of continuous and tragic amazement. The pattern of deception by which the weak circumvent the strong and manage to secure some of their political, economic, and social rights is a matter of continuous degradation. A vast conspiracy of silence covers all these maneuvers as the groups come into contact with each other, and the question of morality is not permitted to invade it.

The tragic consequences of the alternative that there is *no* alternative are not far to seek. In the first place, it tends to destroy whatever sense of ethical values the individual possesses. It is a simple fact of psychology that if a man calls a lie the truth, he tampers dangerously with his value judgments. Jesus called attention to that fact in one of his most revealing utterances. His mother, in an attempt to excuse him from the harsh judgment of his enemies, said that he was a little out of his mind—not terribly crazy, but just a little off-balance. Those who did not like him said that he was all right with regard to his mind, but that he was full of the devil, and that it was by the power of the devil that he was casting out devils. Jesus, hearing the discussion, said that these men did not talk good sense: "A house . . . divided against itself . . . cannot stand." He suggested that if they continued saying that he was casting out devils by the power of the devil—and they knew that such was not the case—they would commit the unpardonable sin. That is to say, if a man continues to call a good thing bad, he will eventually lose his sense of moral distinctions.

Is this always the result? Is it not possible to quarantine a certain kind of deception so that it will not affect the rest of one's life? May not the underprivileged do with deception as it relates to his soul what the human body does with tubercle bacilli? The body seems unable to destroy the bacilli, so nature builds a prison for them, walls them in with a thick fibrosis so that their toxin cannot escape from the lungs into the blood stream. As long as the victim exercises care in the matter of rest, work, and diet, normal activities may be pursued without harm. Is deception a comparable technique of survival, the fibrosis that protects the life from poison in its total outlook or in its other relations? Or, to change the figure, may not deception be regarded under some circumstances as a kind of blind spot that is functional in a limited area of experience? No! Such questions are merely attempts to rationalize one's way out of a critical difficulty.

The penalty of deception is to *become* a deception, with all sense of moral discrimination vitiated. A man who lies habitually becomes a lie, and it is increasingly impossible for him to know when he is lying and when he is not. In other words, the moral mercury of life is reduced to zero. Shakespeare has immortalized this aspect of character in his drama of Macbeth. Macbeth has a high sense of destiny, which is deeply underscored by the testimony of the witches. This is communicated to his wife, who takes it to head and to heart. By a series of liquidations their friends disappear and their enemies multiply, until Macbeth is king and his wife is queen. Together they swim across Scotland in seas of blood, tying laurels on their brows with other people's lives, heartstrings, and hopes. Then fatal things begin happening to them. Lady Macbeth walks in her sleep, trying in vain to wash blood from her hands. But the blood is not on her hands; it is on her soul. Macbeth becomes a victim of terrible visions and he cries:

> Methought I heard a voice cry "Sleep no more!
> Macbeth does murder sleep!" The innocent sleep.

One day, at the most crucial point in Macbeth's life, an attendant announces to him that Lady Macbeth is dead. His reply reveals, in one agonizing flash, the death of values that has taken place in him:

> She should have died hereafter;
> There would have been a time for such a word.
> To-morrow, and to-morrow, and to-morrow,
> Creeps in this petty pace from day to day
> To the last syllable of recorded time,
> And all of our yesterdays have lighted fools
> The way to dusty death. Out, out, brief candle!
> Life's but a walking shadow, a poor player
> That struts and frets his hour upon the stage
> And then is heard no more: it is a tale
> Told by an idiot, full of sound and fury,
> Signifying nothing.

Life is only a tale told by a fool, having no meaning because deception has wiped out all moral distinctions.

The second alternative is a possible derivation from the first one. The underprivileged may decide to juggle the various areas of compromise, on the assumption that the moral quality of compromise operates in an ascending-descending scale. According to this argument, not all issues are equal in significance nor in consequence; it may be that some compromises take on the aspect of inevitability because of circumstances over which the individual has no control. It is true that we are often bound by a network of social relations that operate upon us without being particularly affected by us. We are all affected by forces, social and natural, that in some measure determine our behavior without our being able to bring to bear upon them our private will, however great or righteous it may be.

All over the world there are millions of people who are condemned by the powerful in their society to live in ghettos. The choice seems to be the ghetto or suicide. But such a conclusion may be hasty and ill-advised; it may be the counsel of the kind of fear we discussed previously, or it may be the decision of cowardice. For all practical purposes there are great numbers of people who have decided to *live*, and to compromise on the matter of place and conditions. Further, we may say that those who have power know that the decision will be to live, and have counted on it. They are prepared to deal ruthlessly with any form of effective protest, because effective protest upsets the *status quo*. Life, then, becomes a grim game of wits, and the stakes are one's physical existence.

The term "compromise" then takes on a very special and highly differentiated meaning. It is less positive than ordinary deception, which may be regarded as deliberate strategy. If the assumption is that survival with some measure of freedom is at stake, then compromise is defined in terms of the actions which involve one's life continuation. It is a matter of behavior patterns. Many obvious interferences with freedom are ignored completely. Many insults are cast aside as of no consequence. One does battle only when not to do battle is to be vanquished without the recognition that comes from doing battle. To the morally sensitive person the whole business is sordid and degrading.

67

It is safe to say that the common attitude taken toward these deceptions that have to do with survival is that they are amoral. The moral question is never raised. To raise such a question is regarded as sheer stupidity. The behavior involved is in the same category as seeking and getting food or providing shelter for oneself. It belongs in the general classification of simple survival behavior. Obviously this is the reason why it is so difficult to make a moral appeal, either to the dominant group or to the disinherited, in order to bring about a change in the basic relation between them. For better or for worse, according to this aspect of our analysis, there is no point at which mere moral appeal makes sense. Whatever moral sensitiveness to the situation was present at some stage in the life of the individual has long since been atrophied, due to betrayal, suffering, or frustration.

This alternative, then, must be discussed from the point of view of the observer rather than from that of the victim. The rank and file of the oppressed do not formally raise the questions involved in their behavior. Specifically, the applicability of religion is restricted to those areas in which religious considerations commend themselves as being reasonable. A profound piece of surgery has to take place in the very psyche of the disinherited before the great claim of the religion of Jesus can be presented. The great stretches of barren places in the soul must be revitalized, brought to life, before they can be challenged. Tremendous skill and power must be exercised to show to the disinherited the awful results of the role of negative deception into which their lives have been cast. How to do this is perhaps the greatest challenge that the religion of Jesus faces in modern life.

Mere preaching is not enough. What are words, however sacred and powerful, in the presence of the grim facts of the daily struggle to survive? Any attempt to deal with this situation on a basis of values that disregard the struggle for survival appears to be in itself a compromise with life. It is only when people live in an environment in which they are not required to exert supreme effort into just keeping alive that they seem to be able to select ends besides those of mere physical survival. On the subsistence level, values are interpreted in terms of their bearing upon the one major concern of all activity—not being killed. This is really the form that the dilemma takes. It is not solely a question of keeping the body alive; it is rather how not to be killed. *Not to be killed* becomes the great end, and morality takes its meaning from that center. Until that center is shifted, nothing real can be accomplished. It is the uncanny and perhaps unwitting recognition of this fact that causes those in power to keep the disinherited from participation in meaningful social process. For if the disinherited get such a new center as patriotism, for instance—liberty within the framework of a sense of country or nation—then the aim of *not being killed* is swallowed up by a larger and more transcendent goal. Above all else the disinherited must not have any stake in the social order; they must be made to feel that they are alien, that it is a great boon to be allowed to remain alive, not be exterminated. This was the psychology of the Nazis; it grew out of their theory of the state and the place given the Hebrew people in their ideology. Such is also the attitude of the Ku Klux Klan toward Negroes.

Even within the disinherited group itself artificial and exaggerated emphasis upon not being killed tends to cheapen life. That is to say, the fact that the lives of the disinherited are lightly held by the dominant group tends to create the same attitude among them toward each other.

We come now to the third alternative—a complete and devastating sincerity. I have in my possession a copy of a letter from Mahatma Gandhi to Muriel Lester. The letter says in part: "Speak the truth, without fear and without exception, and see everyone whose work is related to your purpose. You are in God's work, so you need not fear man's scorn. If they listen to your requests and grant them, you will be satisfied. If they reject them, then you must make their rejection your strength." The acceptance of this alternative is to be simply, directly truthful, whatever may be the cost in life, limb, or security. For the individual who accepts this, there may be quick and speedy judgment with attendant loss. But if the number increases and the movement spreads, the vindication of the truth would follow in the wake. There must always be the confidence that the effect of truthfulness can be realized in the mind of the oppressor as well as the oppressed. There is no substitute for such a faith.

Emphasis upon an unwavering sincerity points up at once the major challenge of Jesus to the disinherited and the power of his most revolutionary appeal. "Let your communication be, Yea, yea; Nay, nay: for whatsoever is more than these cometh of evil." "Ye have heard that it hath been said, An eye for an eye, . . . but I say unto you, That ye resist not evil." What does he mean? Does he mean that factors having to do with physical survival are trivial or of no consequence? Is this emphasis merely the counsel of suicide? It seems inescapable that either Jesus was infinitely more realistic than we dare imagine or, taking his words at their face value, he is talking as one who has no understanding of the basic facts of life that touch this central problem. From our analysis of the life of Jesus it seems clear that it was from within the framework of great social pressures upon him and his group that he taught and lived to the very end. It is reasonable to assume, then, that he speaks out of understanding and that his words cannot be lightly disregarded, however devastating they may seem.

It may be argued that the insistence upon complete sincerity has to do only with man's relation to God, not with man's relation to man. To what does such a position lead? Unwavering sincerity says that man should always recognize the fact that he lives always in the presence of God, always under the divine scrutiny, and that there is no really significant living for a man, whatever may be his status, until he has turned and faced the divine scrutiny. Here all men stand stripped to the literal substance of themselves, without disguise, without pretension, without *seeming* whatsoever. No man can fool God. From him nothing is hidden.

Thou compassest my path and my lying down,
and art acquainted with all my ways.
For there is not a word in my tongue,
but, lo, O Lord, thou knowest it altogether. . . .
Whither shall I go from thy spirit?
or whither shall I flee from thy presence?
If I ascend up into heaven, thou art there:
if I make my bed in hell, behold, thou art there. . . .
If I say, Surely the darkness shall cover me;
even the night shall be light about me.
Yea, the darkness hideth not from thee;
but the night shineth as the day:
the darkness and the light are both alike to thee.

Was it against the background of his heritage and his religious faith in the 139th psalm that Jesus assumed his great ethical imperative? This seems to be conclusively brought out in his treatment of the climax of human history. The Judge is on his throne; the sheep are on the right, the goats on the left. The Judge speaks: "I was an hungred, and ye gave me no meat: . . . sick, and in prison, and ye visited me not." The climax of human history is interpreted as a time when the inner significance of men's deeds would be revealed to them. But here a new note is introduced. Sincerity in human relations is equal to, and the same as, sincerity to God. If we accept this explanation as a clue to Jesus' meaning, we come upon the stark fact that the insistence of Jesus upon genuineness is absolute; man's relation to man and man's relation to God are one relation.

A death blow is struck to hypocrisy. One of the major

defense mechanisms of the disinherited is taken away from them. What does Jesus give them in its place? What does he substitute for hypocrisy? Sincerity. But is sincerity a mechanism of defense against the strong? The answer is No. Something more significant takes place. In the presence of an overwhelming sincerity on the part of the disinherited, the dominant themselves are caught with no defense, with the edge taken away from the sense of prerogative and from the status upon which the impregnability of their position rests. They are thrown back upon themselves for their rating. The experience of power has no meaning aside from the other-than-self reference which sustains it. If the position of ascendancy is not acknowledged tacitly and actively by those over whom the ascendancy is exercised, then it falls flat. Hypocrisy on the part of the disinherited in dealing with the dominant group is a tribute yielded by those who are weak. But if this attitude is lacking, or is supplanted by a simple sincerity and genuineness, then it follows that advantage due to the accident of birth or position is reduced to zero. Instead of relation between the weak and the strong there is merely a relationship between human beings. A man is a man, no more, no less. The awareness of this fact marks the supreme moment of human dignity.

CHAPTER FOUR

Hate

HATE is another of the hounds of hell that dog the footsteps of the disinherited in season and out of season. During times of war hatred becomes quite respectable, even though it has to masquerade often under the guise of patriotism. To even the casual observer during the last war it was obvious that the Pearl Harbor attack by the Japanese gave many persons in our country an apparent justification for indulging all of their anticolored feelings. In a Chicago cab, enroute to the University from Englewood, this fact was dramatized for me. The cab had stopped for a red light. Apropos of no conversation the driver turned to me, saying, "Who do they think they are? Those little yellow dogs think they can do that to white men and get away with it!"

During the early days of the war I noticed a definite rise in rudeness and overt expressions of color prejudice, especially in trains and other public conveyances. It was very simple; hatred could be brought out into the open, given a formal dignity and a place of respectability. But for the most part we are not vocal about our hatred. Hating is something of which to be ashamed unless it provides for us a form of validation and prestige. If either is provided, then the immoral or amoral character of the hatred is transformed into positive violence.

Christianity has been almost sentimental in its effort to deal with hatred in human life. It has sought to get rid of hatred by preachments, by moralizing, by platitudinous judgments. It has hesitated to analyze the basis of hatred and to evaluate it in terms of its possible significance in the lives of the people possessed by it. This reluctance to examine hatred has taken on the character of a superstition. It is a subject that is taboo unless there is some extraordinary social crisis—such as war—involving the mobilization of all the national resources of the common life to meet it. There is a conspiracy of silence about hatred, its function and its meaning.

Hatred cannot be defined. It can only be described. If I were to project a simple diagram of hatred, revealing the anatomy of its development, the idea would break down as follows.

In the first place, hatred often begins in a situation in which there is contact without fellowship, contact that is devoid of any of the primary overtures of warmth and fellow-feeling and genuineness. Of course, it must be borne in mind that there can be an abundance of sentimentality masquerading under the cloak of fellowship. It is easy to have fellowship on your own terms and to repudiate it if your terms are not acceptable. It is this kind of fellowship that one finds often in the South between whites and Negroes. As long as the Negro is called John or Mary and accepts the profoundly humiliating position of an inferior status, fellowship is quite possible. Great sacrifices are even made for him, and all the weight of position and power are at the disposal of the weaker person. It is precisely because of this false basis of fellowship so often found that in the section of the country where there is the greatest contact between Negro and white there is the least real fellowship, and the first step along the road of bitterness and hatred is assured.

When we give to the concept a wider application, it is clear that much of modern life is so impersonal that there is always opportunity for the seeds of hatred to grow unmolested. Where there are contacts devoid of genuine fellowship, such contacts stand in immediate candidacy for hatred.

In the second place, contacts without fellowship tend to express themselves in the kind of understanding that is strikingly unsympathetic. There is understanding of a kind, but it is without the healing and reinforcement of personality. Rather, it is like the experience of going into a man's office and, in that moment before being seated, when the full gaze of the other is focused upon you, suddenly wondering whether the top button of your vest is in place, but not daring to look. In a penetrating, incisive, cold understanding there is no cushion to absorb limitations or to provide extenuating circumstances for protection.

76

It is a grievous blunder to assume that understanding is always sympathetic. Very often we use the phrase "I understand" to mean something kindly, warm, and gracious. But there is an understanding that is hard, cold, minute, and deadly. It is the kind of understanding that one gives to the enemy, or that is derived from an accurate knowledge of another's power to injure. There is an understanding of another's weakness, which may be used as a weapon of offense or defense. Understanding that is not the outgrowth of an essential fellow-feeling is likely to be unsympathetic. Of course, there may be pity in it—even compassion, sometimes—but sympathy, almost never. I can sympathize only when I see myself in another's place.

Unsympathetic understanding is the characteristic attitude governing the relation between the weak and the strong. All kinds of first aid may be rendered to the weak; they may be protected so long as there is the abject acknowledgment of their utter dependence upon the strong. When the Southern white person says, "I understand the Negro," what he really means is that he has a knowledge of the Negro within the limitations of the boundaries which the white man has set up. The kind of Negro he understands has no existence except in his own mind.

In the third place, an unsympathetic understanding tends to express itself in the active functioning of ill will. A few years ago I was going from Chicago to Memphis, Tennessee. I found a seat across from an elderly lady, who took immediate cognizance of my presence. When the conductor came along for the tickets, she said to him, pointing in my direction, "What is *that* doing in this car?"

The conductor answered, with a touch of creative humor, "*That* has a ticket."

For the next fifty miles this lady talked for five or ten or fifteen minutes with each person who was seated alone in that coach, setting forth her philosophy of human relationships and the basis of her objection to my presence in the car. I was able to see the atmosphere in the entire car shift from common indifference to active recognition of and, to some extent, positive resentment of my presence; an ill will spreading its virus by contagion.

In the fourth place, ill will, when dramatized in a human being, becomes hatred walking on the earth. The outline is now complete and simple—contacts without fellowship developing hatred and expressing themselves in unsympathetic understanding; an unsympathetic understanding tending to express itself in the exercise of ill will; and ill will, dramatized in a man or woman, becoming hatred walking on the earth.

In many analyses of hatred it is customary to apply it only to the attitude of the strong towards the weak. The general impression is that many white people hate Negroes and that Negroes are merely the victims. Such an assumption is quite ridiculous. I was once seated in a Jim Crow car which extended across the highway at a railway station in Texas. Two Negro girls of about fourteen or fifteen sat behind me. One of them looked out of the window and said, "Look at those kids." She referred to two little white girls, who were skating towards the train. "Wouldn't it be funny if they fell and spattered their brains all over the pavement!" I looked at them. Through what torture chambers had they come—torture chambers that had so attacked the grounds of humaneness in them that there was nothing capable of calling forth any appreciation or understanding of white persons? There was something that made me shiver.

Hatred, in the mind and spirit of the disinherited, is born out of great bitterness—a bitterness that is made possible by sustained resentment which is bottled up until it distills an essence of vitality, giving to the individual in whom this is happening a radical and fundamental basis for self-realization.

Let me illustrate this. Suppose you are one of five children in a family and it happened, again and again, that if there was just enough for four children in any given circumstance, you were the child who had to do without. If there was money for four pairs of shoes and five pairs were needed, it was you who did without shoes. If there were five pieces of cake on the plate, four healthy slices and one small piece, you were given the small slice. At first, when this happened, you overlooked it, because you thought that your sisters and brothers, each in his turn, would have the same experience; but they did not. Then you complained quietly to the brother who was closest to you in understanding, and he thought that you were being disloyal to your mother and father to say such a thing. In a moment of self-righteousness you spoke to your father about it. Your father put you on the carpet so severely that you decided not to mention it again, but you kept on watching. The discrimination continued.

At night, when the lights were out and you were safely tucked away in bed, you reached down into the quiet places of your little heart and lifted out your bundle of hates and resentments growing out of the family situation, and you fingered them gently, one by one. In the darkness you muttered to yourself, "They can keep me from talking about it to them, but they can't keep me from resenting it. I hate them for what they are doing to me. No one can prevent me there." Hatred becomes for you a source of validation for your personality. As you consider the family and their attitude toward you, your hatred gives you a sense of significance which you fling defiantly into the teeth of their estimate of you.

In Herman Melville's *Moby Dick* there is an expression of this attitude. You will doubtless recall the story. Ahab has had his leg bitten off in an encounter with the white whale. He collects a motley crew, and they sail into the northern seas to find and conquer the whale. A storm comes up at sea, and Ahab stands on deck with his ivory leg fastened to the floor. He leans against the railing in utter defiance of the storm. His hair is disheveled, his face is furrowed, and there is a fever in his blood that only the conquest of the white whale can cure. In effect, he says to the lightning, "You may destroy this vessel, you may dry up the bowels of the sea, you may consume me; *but I can still be ashes.*"

It is this kind of attitude that is developed in the mind and soul of the weak and the disinherited. As they look out upon their world, they recognize at once that they are the victims of a systematic denial of the rights and privileges that are theirs, by virtue both of their being human and of their citizenship. Their acute problem is to deal with the estimate that their environment places upon them; for the environment, through its power-controlling and prestige-bearing representatives, has announced to them that they do not rate anything other than that which is being visited upon them. If they accept this judgment, then the grounds of their self-estimate is destroyed, and their acquiescence becomes an endorsement of the judgment of the environment. Because they are despised, they despise themselves. If they reject the judgment, hatred may serve as a device for rebuilding, step by perilous step, the foundation for individual significance; so that from within the intensity of their necessity they declare their right to exist, despite the judgment of the environment.

I remember that once, when moving from one home to another, I came upon a quiet family of mice in a box in the basement. Their presence created a moral problem for me, for I did not feel that I had the right to take their lives. Then I remembered my responsibility to the family that was moving in, and, with heaviness of heart, I took my daughter's little broom and descended upon them with a mighty stroke. Sensing the impending tragedy, one of them raised himself on his haunches to meet the stroke of the broom with a squeal of defiance, affirming the core of his mouse integrity in the face of descending destruction. Hatred makes this sort of profound contribution to the life of the disinherited, because it establishes a dimension of self-realization hammered out of the raw materials of injustice.

A distinct derivative from hatred's contribution to self-realization, when self-realization is established as a rallying point for the personality, is the tremendous source of dynamic energy provided. Surplus energy is created and placed at the disposal of the individual's needs and ends. In a sense the whole personality is alerted. All kinds of supports for implementing one's affirmed position are seized upon. A strange, new cunning possesses the mind, and every opportunity for taking advantage, for defeating the enemy, is revealed in clear perspective. One of the salient ways by which this expresses itself is the quality of endurance that appears. It is the sort of thing that causes a little boy, when he is being overpowered by a big boy, to refrain from tears or from giving any expression that will reveal the depths of his pain and hurt. He says to himself grimly, "I'll die before I cry."

I have already pointed out that the relationship between the strong and the weak is characterized often by its amoral aspect. When hatred serves as a dimension of self-realization, the illusion of righteousness is easy to create. Often there are but thin lines between bitterness, hatred, self-realization, defiance, and righteous indignation. The logic of the strong-weak relationship is to place all moral judgment of behavior out of bounds. A type of behavior that, under normal circumstances, would call for self-condemnation can very easily, under these special circumstances, be regarded as necessary and therefore defensible. To take advantage of the strong is regarded merely as settling an account. It is open season all the time, without the operation of normal moral inhibitions. It is a form of the old *lex talionis*—eye for an eye, tooth for a tooth.

Thus hatred becomes a device by which an individual seeks to protect himself against moral disintegration. He does to other human beings what he could not ordinarily do to them without losing his self-respect. This is an aspect of hatred that has almost universal application during a time of war and national crisis. Doubtless you will recall that during the last war a very interesting defense of hatred appeared in America. The reasoning ran something like this: American boys have grown up in a culture and a civilization in which they have absorbed certain broad attitudes of respect for human personality, and other traits characteristic of gentlemen of refinement and dignity. Therefore they are not prepared psychologically or emotionally to become human war machines, to make themselves conscious instruments of death. Something radical has to happen to their personality and their over-all outlook to render them more effective tools of destruction. The most effective way by which this transformation can be brought about is through discipline in hatred; for if they hate the enemy, then that hatred will immunize them from a loss of moral self-respect as they do to the enemy what is demanded of them in the successful prosecution of the war.

To use a figure, a curtain was dropped in front of their moral values and their ethical integrity as human beings and Americans, and they moved around in front of that curtain to do their death-dealing work on other human beings. The curtain of protection was the disciplined hatred. A simple illustration of what I mean is this: There are some people who cannot tell you face to face precisely what they think of you unless they get angry first. Anger serves as a protection of their finer sense of values as they look you in the eye and say things which, under ordinary circumstances, they would not be able to say.

When I was a boy, my mother occasionally found it necessary to punish me and my sister. My sister, when whipped, would look my mother in the face, showing no visible signs of emotional reaction. This attitude caused the burden of proof to shift from her shoulders to my mother's shoulders, with the result that my mother did not whip my sister with such intensity growing out of self-righteous indignation as if the reaction had been otherwise. When my turn came, all the neighbors knew what was happening in the Thurman family. Therefore my mother whipped me with an attention to detail that was radically different from the experience she had with my sister. My attitude fed her indignation to the point of giving her complete immunity from self-condemnation. This is precisely what hatred does in human beings faced with hard and brutal choices in dealing with each other.

It is not difficult to see how hatred, operating in this fashion, provides for the weak a basis for moral justification. Every expression of intolerance, every attitude of meanness, every statute that limits and degrades, gives further justification for life-negation on the part of the weak toward the strong. It makes possible for an individual to be life-affirming and life-negating at one and the same time. If a man's attitude is life-negating in his relationships with those to whom he recognizes no moral responsibility, his conduct is without condemnation in his own mind. In his relations with his fellows to whom he recognizes moral responsibility, his attitude is life-affirming. There must be within him some guarantee against contagion by the life-negating attitude, lest he lose a sense of moral integrity in all of his relationships. Hatred seems to function as such a guarantee. The oppressed can give themselves over with utter enthusiasm to life-affirming attitudes toward their fellow sufferers, and this becomes compensation for their life-negating attitude toward the strong.

Of course, back of this whole claim of logic is the idea that there is a fundamental justice in life, upon which the human spirit in its desperation may rely. In its more beatific definition it is the basis of the composure of the martyr who is being burned at the stake; he seems to be caught up in the swirl of elemental energy and power that transforms the weakness and limitation of his personality into that which makes of him a superhuman being.

It is clear, then, that for the weak, hatred seems to serve a creative purpose. It may be judged harshly by impersonal ethical standards, but as long as the weak see it as being inextricably involved in the complicated technique of survival with dignity, it cannot easily be dislodged. Jesus understood this. What must have passed through his mind when he observed the contemptuous disregard for the Jews by the Romans, whose power had closed in on Israel? What thoughts raced through his mind when Judas of Galilee raised his rallying banner of defiance, sucking into the tempest of his embittered spirit many of the sons of Judah? Is it reasonable to assume that Jesus did not understand the anatomy of hatred? In the face of the obvious facts of his environment he counseled against hatred, and his word is, "Love your enemies, . . . that ye may be the children of your Father which is in heaven: for he maketh his sun to rise on the evil and on the good, and sendeth rain on the just and the unjust." Why?

Despite all the positive psychological attributes of hatred we have outlined, hatred destroys finally the core of the life of the hater. While it lasts, burning in white heat, its effect seems positive and dynamic. But at last it turns to ash, for it guarantees a final isolation from one's fellows. It blinds the individual to all values of worth, even as they apply to himself and to his fellows. Hatred bears deadly and bitter fruit. It is blind and nondiscriminating. True, it begins by exercising specific discrimination. This it does by centering upon the persons responsible for the situations which create the reaction of resentment, bitterness, and hatred. But once hatred is released, it cannot be confined to the offenders alone. It is difficult for hatred to be informed as to objects when it gets under way. I remember that when I was an undergraduate in Atlanta, Georgia, a man came into the president's office, in which I was the errand boy. The president was busy, so the man engaged me in conversation. Eventually he began talking about his two little boys. He said, among other things, "I am rearing my boys so that they will not hate Negroes. Do not misunderstand me. I do not love them, but I am wise enough to know that if I teach my boys to hate Negroes, they will end up hating white people as well." Hatred cannot be controlled once it is set in motion.

Some years ago a medical friend of mine gave me a physical examination. After weighing me he said, "You'd better watch your weight. You are getting up in years now, and your weight will have a bad effect on your vital organs." He explained this in graphic detail. While he was talking, I chuckled; for, as I looked at him, I saw a man about 5 feet 4 inches in height who weighed 215 pounds. My friend, the doctor, thought his body knew that he was a doctor. But his body did not know he was a doctor; the only thing it knew was that he was accumulating more energy through his food than his body was able to consume. Hence his body did precisely what mine was doing. It stored energy in the form of fat.

Hatred is like that. It does not know anything about the pressures exerted upon the weak by the strong. It knows nothing about the extentuating circumstances growing out of a period of national crisis, making it seemingly necessary to discipline men in hatred of other human beings. The terrible truth remains. The logic of the development of hatred is death to the spirit and disintegration of ethical and moral values.

Above and beyond all else it must be borne in mind that hatred tends to dry up the springs of creative thought in the life of the hater, so that his resourcefulness becomes completely focused on the negative aspects of his environment. The urgent needs of the personality for creative expression are starved to death. A man's horizon may become so completely dominated by the intense character of his hatred that there remains no creative residue in his mind and spirit to give to great ideas, to great concepts. He becomes lopsided. To use the phrase from Zarathurstra, he becomes "a cripple in reverse."

Jesus rejected hatred. It was not because he lacked the vitality or the strength. It was not because he lacked the incentive. Jesus rejected hatred because he saw that hatred meant death to the mind, death to the spirit, death to communion with his Father. He affirmed life; and hatred was the great denial. To him it was clear

> Thou must not make division.
> Thy mind, heart, soul and strength must ever search
> To find the way by which the road
> To all men's need of thee must go.
> This is the Highway of the Lord.[1]

[1] From my privately published volume of poems, *The Greatest of These*, p. 9.

CHAPTER FIVE

Love

THE religion of Jesus makes the love-ethic central. This is no ordinary achievement. It seems clear that Jesus started out with the simple teaching concerning love embodied in the timeless words of Israel: "Hear, O Israel: The Lord our God is one Lord: and thou shalt love the Lord thy God with all thy heart, and with all thy soul, and with all thy might," and "thy neighbour as thyself." Once the neighbor is defined, then one's moral obligation is clear. In a memorable story Jesus defined the neighbor by telling of the Good Samaritan. With sure artistry and great power he depicted what happens when a man responds directly to human need across the barriers of class, race, and condition. Every man is potentially every other man's neighbor. Neighborliness is nonspatial; it is qualitative. A man must love his neighbor directly, clearly, permitting no barriers between.

This was not an easy position for Jesus to take within his own community. Opposition to his teaching increased as the days passed. A twofold demand was made upon him at all times: to love those of the household of Israel who became his enemies because they regarded him as a careless perverter of the truths of God; to love those beyond the household of Israel—the Samaritan, and even the Roman.

The former demand was deeply dramatized by the fact that Jesus did not consider himself as one who stood outside of Israel. If he had regarded himself as one who was starting a new religion, a new faith, then it would not have been hard to account for bitter opposition. With justice, the defenders of the faith could have opposed him because he would have been deliberately trying to destroy the very grounds of Judaism. But if it be true—as I think it is—that Jesus felt he was merely serving as a creative vehicle for the authentic genius of Israel, completely devoted to the will of God, then in order to love those of the household he must conquer his own pride. In their attitude he seemed to see the profoundest betrayal of the purpose of God. It is curious that as each looked on the other the accusations were identical.

In the second place, Jesus had to deal with the Samaritans in working out the application of his love-ethic. His solution of this bitter problem is found in the story of the Good Samaritan. There is also the very instructive account of the interview between Jesus and the Syrophoenician woman.

Opposition to the interpretation which Jesus was giving to the gospel of God had increased, and Jesus and his disciples withdrew from active work into temporary semi-retirement around Tyre and Sidon. The woman broke into his retreat with an urgent request in behalf of her child. Jesus said to her, "It is not meet to take the children's bread, and cast it to dogs." This was more a probing query than an affirmation. It had in it all the deep frustration which he had experienced, and there flashed through it generations of religious exclusiveness to which he was heir. "What right has this woman of another race to make a claim upon me? What mockery is there here? Am I not humiliated enough in being misunderstood by my own kind? And here this woman dares to demand that which, in the very nature of the case, she cannot claim as her due."

Into the riotous thoughts that were surging in his mind her voice struck like a bolt of lightning: "Truth, Lord: yet the dogs eat of the crumbs which fall from their masters' table."

"Go—go, woman, go in peace; your faith hath saved you."

But this was not all. Jesus had to apply his love-ethic to the enemy—to the Roman, the ruler. This was the hardest task, because to tamper with the enemy was to court disaster. To hate him in any way that caused action was to invite the wrath of Rome. To love him was to be regarded as a traitor to Jesus' own people, to Israel, and therefore to God. As was suggested in the first chapter, it was upon the anvil of the Jewish community's relations with Rome that Jesus hammered out the vital content of his concept of love for one's enemy.

"The enemy" can very easily be divided into three groups. There is first the personal enemy, one who is in

some sense a part of one's primary-group life. The relationship with such a person is grounded in more or less intimate, personal associations into which has entered conflict.
Such conflict may have resulted from misunderstanding or
from harsh words growing out of a hot temper and too
much pride on either side to make amends. It may have
come about because of an old family feud by which those
who were never a part of the original rift are victimized.
The strained relationship may have been due to the evil
work of a vicious tongue. The point is that the enemy in
this sense is one who at some time was a rather intimate
part of one's world and was close enough to be taken into
account in terms of intimacy.

To love such an enemy requires reconciliation, the will
to re-establish a relationship. It involves confession of error
and a seeking to be restored to one's former place. Doubtless
it is this that Jesus had in mind in his charge: "If thou
bring thy gift to the altar, and there rememberest that thy
brother hath ought against thee; leave there thy gift before
the altar, . . . and go be reconciled to thy brother and then
come and offer thy gift."

It is with this kind of enemy that the disinherited find
it easiest to deal. They accept with good grace the insistence
of Jesus that they deal with the rifts in their own world.
Here, they are at the center; they count specifically, and
their wills are crucial. When one analyzes the preaching and
the religious teachings in the churches of his country, he discovers that the term "enemy" usually has this rather restricted meaning. When the Negro accepts the teaching of

love, it is this narrow interpretation which is uppermost. I grew up with this interpretation. I dare to say that, in the white churches in my little town, the youths were trained in the same narrow interpretation applied to white persons. Love those who have a natural claim upon you. To those who have no such claim, there is no responsibility.

The second kind of enemy comprises those persons who, by their activities, make it difficult for the group to live without shame and humiliation. It does not require much imagination to assume that to the sensitive son of Israel the taxgatherers were in that class. It was they who became the grasping hand of Roman authority, filching from Israel the taxes which helped to keep alive the oppression of the gentile ruler. They were Israelites who understood the psychology of the people, and therefore were always able to function with the kind of spiritual ruthlessness that would have been impossible for those who did not know the people intimately. They were despised; they were outcasts, because from the inside they had unlocked the door to the enemy. The situation was all the more difficult to bear because the tax collectors tended to be prosperous in contrast with the rest of the people. To be required to love such a person was the final insult. How could such a demand be made? One did not even associate with such creatures. To be seen in their company meant a complete loss of status and respect in the community. The taxgatherer had no soul; he had long since lost it. When Jesus became a friend to the tax collectors and secured one as his intimate companion, it was a spiritual triumph of such staggering proportions that after nineteen hundred years it defies rational explanation.

The argument for loving this second enemy was the fact that he too was a son of Abraham. He was one of them, unworthy though he was. Here was the so-called call of blood, which cannot be stilled. God required that Israel be one people, even as he was one.

All underprivileged people have to deal with this kind of enemy. There are always those who seem to be willing to put their special knowledge at the disposal of the dominant group to facilitate the tightening of the chains. They are given position, often prominence, and above all a guarantee of economic security and status. To love such people requires the uprooting of the bitterness of betrayal, the heartiest poison that grows in the human spirit. There must be some understanding of how such people become as they are. Is it because they are weak and must build their strength by feeding upon the misery of their fellows? Is it because they want power and, recognizing the fact that they can never compete within the group for a place of significance, are thus driven by some strange inner urge to get by cunning what they cannot secure by integrity? Is it because they resent the circumstances of their birth and fling their defiance into the teeth of life by making everything foul and unclean within the reach of their contact and power?

There is no simple or single answer. In every ghetto, in every dwelling place of the disinherited throughout the ages, these persons have appeared. To love them means to recognize some deep respect and reverence for their persons.

But to love them does not mean to condone their way of life.

Jesus demonstrated that the only way to redeem them for the common cause was to penetrate their thick resistance to public opinion and esteem and lay bare the simple heart. This man is not just a tax collector; he is a son of God. Awaken that awareness in him and he will attack his betrayal as only he can—from the inside. It was out of this struggle and triumph that Jesus says: "Love your enemies, do good to them which hate you." Hence he called Matthew, the tax collector, to follow him.

The third type of enemy was exemplified by Rome. The elements at work here were both personal and impersonal; they were religious and political. To deal with Rome as a moral enemy required a spiritual recognition of the relationship with the empire. This was made even more precarious because of the development of the cult of emperor worship. But Rome was the political enemy. To love the Roman meant first to lift him out of the general classification of enemy. The Roman had to emerge as a person.

On the surface this would not be too difficult. The basic requirement was that the particular Roman be established in some primary, face-to-face relationship of gross equality. There had to be a moment when the Roman and the Jew emerged as neither Roman nor Jew, but as two human spirits that had found a mutual, though individual, validation. For the most part, such an experience would be impossible as long as either was functioning only within his own social context. The Roman, viewed against the background of his nation and its power, was endowed in the mind of the Jew with all the arrogance and power of the dominant group. It would matter not how much the individual wished to be regarded for himself alone or to be permitted to disassociate himself from all the entangling embarrassments of his birthright; the fact remained always present. He was a Roman and had to bear on his shoulders the full weight of that responsibility. If he tried to make common cause with the Jew, he was constantly under suspicion, and was never to be trusted and taken all the way into the confidence of the other.

Of course, the Jewish person was under the same handicap. It was almost impossible for him to emerge as a person; always in the background was the fact of difference and the disadvantage of status. If he wanted to know the Roman for himself, he ran the risk of being accused by his fellows of consorting with the enemy. If he persisted, it would be simply a matter of time before he would be regarded as an enemy and forced to take the consequences. The more he explained his motives, the deep ethical and spiritual urgency which forced the irregular behavior, the more hypocritical he would seem.

Once isolation from one's fellows has been achieved, one is at the mercy of doubts, fears, and confusion. One might say, "Suppose I have misread the will of God. Suppose I am really acting in this way because I do not have the courage to hate. Suppose those I am learning to love turn and rend me with added contempt and condescension. Then what? Does it mean that God has failed me? Does it mean that there is, at long last, no ultimate integrity in the ethical enterprise? Does it mean that the love ideal is so absolute that it vitiates something as frail and limited as human life— that thus it is an evil and not a good? 'My God, my God, why hast thou forsaken me?' "

Love of the enemy means that a fundamental attack must first be made on the enemy status. How can this be done? Does it mean merely ignoring the fact that he belongs to the enemy class? Hardly. For lack of a better term, an "unscrambling" process is required. Obviously a situation has to be set up in which it is possible for primary contacts to be multiplied. By this I do not mean contacts that are determined by status or by social distinctions. There are always primary contacts between the weak and the strong, the privileged and the underprivileged, but they are generally contacts within zones of agreement which leave the status of the individual intact. There is great intimacy between whites and Negroes, but it is usually between servant and served, between employer and employee. Once the status of each is frozen or fixed, contacts are merely truces between enemies—a kind of armistice for purposes of economic security. True, there are times when something great and dependable emerges, and the miracle takes place even though the status has remained, formally. But during such moments status is merely transcended; it is not broken down. If it is transcended over a time interval of sufficient duration, a permanent emergence takes place. But, in a very tragic sense, the ultimate fate of the relationship seems to be in the hands of the wider social context.

97

It is necessary, therefore, for the privileged and the underprivileged to work on the common environment for the purpose of providing normal experiences of fellowship. This is one very important reason for the insistence that segregation is a complete ethical and moral evil. Whatever it may do for those who dwell on either side of the wall, one thing is certain: it poisons all normal contacts of those persons involved. The first step toward love is a common sharing of a sense of mutual worth and value. This cannot be discovered in a vacuum or in a series of artificial or hypothetical relationships. It has to be in a real situation, natural, free.

The experience of the common worship of God is such a moment. It is in this connection that American Christianity has betrayed the religion of Jesus almost beyond redemption. Churches have been established for the underprivileged, for the weak, for the poor, on the theory that they prefer to be among themselves. Churches have been established for the Chinese, the Japanese, the Korean, the Mexican, the Filipino, the Italian, and the Negro, with the same theory in mind. The result is that in the one place in which normal, free contacts might be most naturally established—in which the relations of the individual to his God should take priority over conditions of class, race, power, status, wealth, or the like—this place is one of the chief instruments for guaranteeing barriers.

It is in order to quote these paragraphs from a recently published book, *The Protestant Church and the Negro*, by Frank S. Loescher:

There are approximately 8,000,000 Protestant Negroes. About 7,500,000 are in separate Negro denominations. Therefore, from the local church through the regional organizations to the national assemblies over 93 per cent of the Negroes are without association in work and worship with Christians of other races except in interdenominational organizations which involves a few of their leaders. The remaining 500,000 Negro Protestants—about 6 per cent—are in predominantly white denominations, and of these 500,000 Negroes in "white" churches, at least 99 per cent, judging by the surveys of six denominations, are in segregated congregations. They are in association with their white denominational brothers only in national assemblies, and, in some denominations, in regional, state, or more local jursdictional meetings. There remains a handful of Negro members in local "white" churches. How many? Call it one-tenth of one per cent of all the Negro Protestant Christians in the United States—8,000 souls—the figure is probably much too large. Whatever the figure actually is, the number of white and Negro persons who ever gather together for worship under the auspices of Protestant Christianity is almost microscopic. And where interracial worship does occur, it is, for the most part, in communities where there are only a few Negro families and where, therefore, only a few Negro individuals are available to "white" churches.

That is the over-all picture, a picture which hardly reveals the Protestant church as a dynamic agency in the integration of American Negroes into American life. Negro membership appears to be confined to less than one per cent of the local "white" churches, usually churches in small communities where but a few Negroes live and have already experienced a high degree of integration by other community institutions—communities one might add where it is unsound to establish a Negro church since Negroes are in such small numbers. It is an even smaller percentage of white churches in which Negroes are reported to be participating freely, or are integrated.

The same pattern appears to be true for other colored minorities, that is, Japanese, Chinese, Indians, Mexicans, Puerto Ricans. Regarding the Mexicans and Puerto Ricans, for example, a director of home missions work in a great denomination says his experience leads him to believe that "generally there is little, if any, discrimination here though in a community which has a large Mexican population it is quite true that they have their own churches." [1]

The enormity of this sin cannot be easily grasped. The situation is so tragic that men of good will in all the specious classifications within our society find more cause for hope in the secular relations of life than in religion.

The religion of Jesus says to the disinherited: "Love your enemy. Take the initiative in seeking ways by which you can have the experience of a common sharing of mutual worth and value. It may be hazardous, but you must do it." For the Negro it means that he must see the individual white man in the context of a common humanity. The fact that a particular individual is white, and therefore may be regarded in some over-all sense as the racial enemy, must be faced; and opportunity must be provided, found, or created for freeing such an individual from his "white necessity." From this point on, the relationship becomes like any other primary one.

Once an attack is made on the enemy status and the individual has emerged, the underprivileged man must him-

[1] Pp. 76-78.

self be status free. It may be argued that his sense of freedom must come first. Here I think the answer may be determined by the one who initiates the activity. But in either case love is possible only between two freed spirits. What one discovers in even a single experience in which barriers have been removed may become useful in building an over-all technique for loving one's enemy. There cannot be too great insistence on the point that we are here dealing with a discipline, a method, a technique, as over against some form of wishful thinking or simple desiring.

Once the mutual discovery is made that the privileged is a man and the underprivileged is a man, or that the Negro is a man and the white man is a man, then the normal desire to make this discovery inclusive of all brings one to grips with the necessity for working out a technique of implementation. The underprivileged man cannot get to know many people as he knows one individual, and yet he is in constant contact with many, in ways that deepen the conflict. Is there some skill which may be applied at a moment's notice that will make a difference even in the most casual relationships? Such a technique may be found in the attitude of respect for personality.

Preliminary to any discussion of the significance of this attitude, some urgent word of caution must be given. For the most part the relationship between the weak and the strong is basically amoral, or it is characterized by a facile use of the mood of "the exception." It is easy to say about a particular individual, "He is different," or, "He is exceptional," and to imply that the general rule or the general attitude does not apply.

This mood of exception operates in still another way. A whole group may be regarded as an exception, and thus one is relieved of any necessity to regard them as human beings. A Negro may say: "If a man is white, he may be automatically classified as one incapable of dealing with me as if he were a rational human being." Or it may be just the reverse. Such a mood, the mood of exception, operates in all sorts of ways. A Republican may say the same thing about a Socialist. The deadly consequences of this attitude are evident. On the same principle scapegoats are provided, upon whose helpless heads we pour our failures and our fears.

The attitude of respect for personality presupposes that all the individuals involved are within what may be called the ethical field. The privileged man must be regarded as being within the area in which ethical considerations are mandatory. If either privileged or underprivileged is out of bounds, the point has no validity.

It is important now to ask how Jesus used this attitude. How did he spell it out? One day a Roman captain came to him seeking help for his servant, for whom he had a profound attachment—a Roman citizen seeking help from a Jewish teacher! Deep was his anguish and distress; all other sources of help had failed. That which would have been expected in the attitude of the Roman growing out of the disjointed relationship between them and the Jews was conspicuously lacking here. The fact that he had come to Jesus was in itself evidence to warrant the conclusion that he had put aside the pride of race and status which would have caused him to regard himself as superior to Jesus. He placed his need directly and simply before Jesus, saying, "Lord, my servant lieth at home sick of the palsy, grievously tormented." By implication he says, "It is my faith that speaks, that cries out. I am stripped bare of all pretense and false pride. The man in me appeals to the man in you." So great was his faith and his humility that when Jesus said that he would come to his home, the captain replied, "I am not worthy that thou shouldest come under my roof; but speak the word only, and my servant shall be healed."

It was the testimony of Jesus that he had found no such faith in all Israel. The Roman was confronted with an insistence that made it impossible for him to remain a Roman, or even a captain. He had to take his place alongside all the rest of humanity and mingle his desires with the longing of all the desperate people of all the ages. When this happened, it was possible at once for him to scale with Jesus any height of understanding, fellowship, and love. The final barrier between the strong and the weak, between ruler and ruled, disappeared.

In the casual relationships between the privileged and the underprivileged there may not be many occurrences of so dramatic a character. Naturally. The average underprivileged man is not a Jesus of Nazareth. The fact remains, however, that wherever a need is laid bare, those who stand in the presence of it can be confronted with the experience of universality that makes all class and race distinctions impertinent. During the great Vanport, Oregon, disaster, when rising waters left thousands homeless, many people of Portland who, prior to that time were sure of their "white supremacy," opened their homes to Negroes, Mexicans, and Japanese. The result was that they were all confronted with the experience of universality. They were no longer white, black, and brown. They were men, women, and children in the presence of the operation of impersonal Nature. Under the pressure they were the human family, and each stood in immediate candidacy for the profoundest fellowship, understanding, and love.

In many experiences of the last war this primary discovery was made. Since an army is a part of the pretensions of the modern state, the state's using it to perpetuate the system of segregation is mere stupidity. The multiplication of moments when citizens—in this instance soldiers—may be confronted with an experience of universality is simply staggering. Aside from all consideration of the issues of war and peace, here is a public activity of the state in which the raw material of democracy can be fashioned into an experience of that personality confirmation without which there can be no lasting health in the state. It is not merely coincidental that this same experience is that out of which the ethical premise of love can find fulfillment.

The concept of reverence for personality, then, is applicable between persons from whom, in the initial instance, the heavy weight of status has been sloughed off. Then what? Each person meets the other where he is and there treats him as if he were where he ought to be. Here we emerge into an area where love operates, revealing a universal characteristic unbounded by special or limited circumstances.

How did Jesus define it? One day a woman was brought to Jesus. She had been caught in the act of adultery. The spokesman for the group who brought her said she was caught red-handed and that according to the law she should be stoned to death. "What is your judgment?" was their searching question. To them the woman was not a woman, or even a person, but an adulteress, stripped of her essential dignity and worth. Said Jesus: "He that is without sin among you, let him first cast a stone." After that, he implied, any person may throw. The quiet words exploded the situation, and in the piercing glare each man saw himself in his literal substance. In that moment each was not a judge of another's deeds, but of his own. In the same glare the adulteress saw herself merely as a woman involved in the meshes of a struggle with her own elemental passion.

Jesus, always the gentleman, did not look at the woman as she stood before him. Instead, he looked on the ground, busied himself with his thoughts. What a moment, reaching beyond time into eternity!

Jesus waited. One by one the men crept away. The woman alone was left. Hearing no outcry, Jesus raised his eyes and beheld the woman. "Where are those thine accusers? hath no man condemned thee?"

"No man, Lord."

"Neither do I condemn thee: go, and sin no more."

This is how Jesus demonstrated reverence for personality. He met the woman where she was, and he treated her as if she were already where she now willed to be. In dealing with her he "believed" her into the fulfillment of her possibilities. He stirred her confidence into activity. He placed a crown over her head which for the rest of her life she would keep trying to grow tall enough to wear.

> Free at last, free at last.
> Thank God Almighty, I'm free at last.

The crucial question is, Can this attitude, developed in the white heat of personal encounter, become characteristic of one's behavior even when the drama of immediacy is lacking? I think so. It has to be rooted in concrete experience. No amount of good feeling for people in general, no amount of simple desiring, is an adequate substitute. It is the act of inner authority, well within the reach of everyone. Obviously, then, merely preaching love of one's enemies or exhortations—however high and holy—cannot, in the last analysis, accomplish this result. At the center of the attitude is a core of painstaking discipline, made possible only by personal triumph. The ethical demand upon the more privileged and the underprivileged is the same.

There is another aspect of the problem which is crucial for the disinherited who is seeking in his love to overcome his hatred. The disinherited man has a sense of gross injury. He finds it well-nigh impossible to forgive, because his injury is often gratuitous. It is not for something that he has done, an action resulting from a deliberate violation of another. He is penalized for what he *is* in the eyes and the standards of another. Somehow he must free himself of the will to retaliation that keeps alive his hatred. Years ago I heard an American missionary to Arabia make a speech concerning the attitude of the people in that land toward the British. He said that he and an Arab friend were taking a boat ride down a certain river when a British yacht passed. With quiet fury the Arab friend said, "Damn the English."

"Why do you say that? They have done good service to your country in terms of health and so forth. I don't understand."

"I said, 'Damn the English,' because they think they are better than I am." Here was stark bitterness fed by the steady oozing of the will to resentment.

It is clear that before love can operate, there is the necessity for forgiveness of injury perpetuated against a person by a group. This is the issue for the disinherited. Once again the answer is not simple. Perhaps there is no answer that is completely satisfying from the point of view of rational reflection. Can the mouse forgive the cat for eating him? It does seem that Jesus dealt with every act of forgiveness as one who was convinced that there is in every act of injury an element that is irresponsible and irrational. No evil deed—and no good deed, either—was named by him as an expression of the total mind of the doer. Once, when someone addressed him as "Good Master," Jesus is quoted as having said, "Why callest thou me good? there is none good, but . . . God."

In Jesus' insistence that we should forgive seventy times seven, there seems to be the assumption that forgiveness is mandatory for three reasons. First, God forgives us again and again for what we do intentionally and unintentionally. There is present an element that is contingent upon our attitude. Forgiveness beyond this is interpreted as the work of divine grace. Second, no evil deed represents the full intent of the doer. Third, the evildoer does not go unpunished. Life is its own restraint. In the wide sweep of the ebb and flow of moral law our deeds track us down, and doer and deed meet. "Vengeance is mine; I will repay, saith the Lord." At the moment of injury or in the slow burning fires of resentment this may be poor comfort. This is the ultimate ground in which finally a profound, unrelieved injury is absorbed. When all other means have been exhausted, each in his own tongue whispers, "There *is* forgiveness with God."

What, then, is the word of the religion of Jesus to those who stand with their backs against the wall? There must be the clearest possible understanding of the anatomy of the issues facing them. They must recognize fear, deception, hatred, each for what it is. Once having done this, they must learn how to destroy these or to render themselves immune to their domination. In so great an undertaking it will become increasingly clear that the contradictions of life are not ultimate. The disinherited will know for themselves that there is a Spirit at work in life and in the hearts of men which is committed to overcoming the world. It is universal, knowing no age, no race, no culture, and no condition of men. For the privileged and underprivileged alike, if the individual puts at the disposal of the Spirit the needful dedication and discipline, he can live effectively in the chaos of the present the high destiny of a son of God.

Epilogue

For every man there is a necessity to establish as securely as possible the lines along which he proposes to live his life. In developing his life's working paper he must take into account many factors, in his reaction to which he may seem to throw them out of line with their true significance. As a man he did not happen. He was born; he has a name; he has forebears; he is the product of a particular culture; he has a mother tongue; he belongs to a nation; he is born into some kind of faith. In addition to all of these he exists in some curious way as a person independent of all other facts. There is an intensely private world, all his own; it is intimate, exclusive, sealed.

The life working paper of the individual is made up of a creative synthesis of what the man is in all his parts and how he reacts to the living process. It is wide of the mark to say that a man's working paper is ever wrong; it may not be fruitful, it may be negative, but it is never wrong. For such a judgment would imply that the synthesis is

110

guaranteed to be of a certain kind, of a specific character, resulting in a foreordained end.

It can never be determined just what a man will fashion. Two men may be born of the same parents, grow up in the same environment, be steeped in the same culture and inspired by the same faith. Close or even cursory observation may reveal that each has fashioned a life working paper so unique that they take to different roads, each day bringing them farther and farther apart. Or it may be that they move along precisely parallel lines that never meet.

Always, then, there is the miracle of the working paper. Wherever there appears in human history a personality whose story is available and whose reach extends far, in all directions, the question of his working paper is as crucial as is the significance of his life. We want to know what were the lines along which he decided to live his life. How did he relate himself to the central issues of his time? What were the questions which he had to answer? Was he under some necessity to give a universal character to his most private experience?

Our attention is called to such a figure because of the impact which his life makes upon human history. For what is human history but man's working paper as he rides high to life caught often in the swirling eddies of tremendous impersonal forces set in motion by vast impulses out of the womb of the Eternal. When a solitary individual is able to mingle his strength with the forces of history and emerge with a name, a character, a personality, it is no ordinary achievement. It is more than the fact that there is a record of his life—as singular as that fact may be. It means that against the background of anonymity he has emerged articulate, and particular.

Such a figure was Jesus of Nazareth. To some he is the grand prototype of all the distilled longing of mankind for fulfillment, for wholeness, for perfection. To some he is the Eternal Presence hovering over all the myriad needs of humanity, yielding healing for the sick of body and soul, giving a lift to those whom weariness has overtaken in the long march, and calling out hidden purposes of destiny which are the common heritage. To some he is more than a Presence; he is the God fact, the Divine Moment in human sin and human misery. To still others he is a man who found the answer to life's riddle, and out of a profound gratitude he becomes the Man most worthy of honor and praise. For such his answer becomes humanity's answer and his life the common claim. In him the miracle of the working paper is writ large, for what he did all men may do. Thus interpreted, he belongs to no age, no race, no creed. When men look into his face, they see etched the glory of their own possibilities, and their hearts whisper, "Thank you and thank God!"